LONG AGO IN PEAKLAND

By

M. ANDREWS, M.B.E.
(*Member of the Derbyshire Arch. Soc.*)

AUTHOR OF "*Jack o' Winnats,*"
"*Story of Old Scarbro,*"
"*O Little Filey,*" etc.

R. MILWARD & SONS, LTD.
LEENGATE, LENTON
NOTTINGHAM

A copy of the first edition was graciously accepted by Her Majesty Queen Elizabeth The Queen Mother.

1st Edition	—August 1948
2nd Edition	—September 1948
3rd Edition	—(Revised) 1950
4th Edition	—(Revised) 1955 with new photographs
5th Edition	—1961
6th Edition	—1966
7th Edition	—1970

Frontispiece
THE LONG CAUSEWAY
(by courtesy of Messrs. Northend).

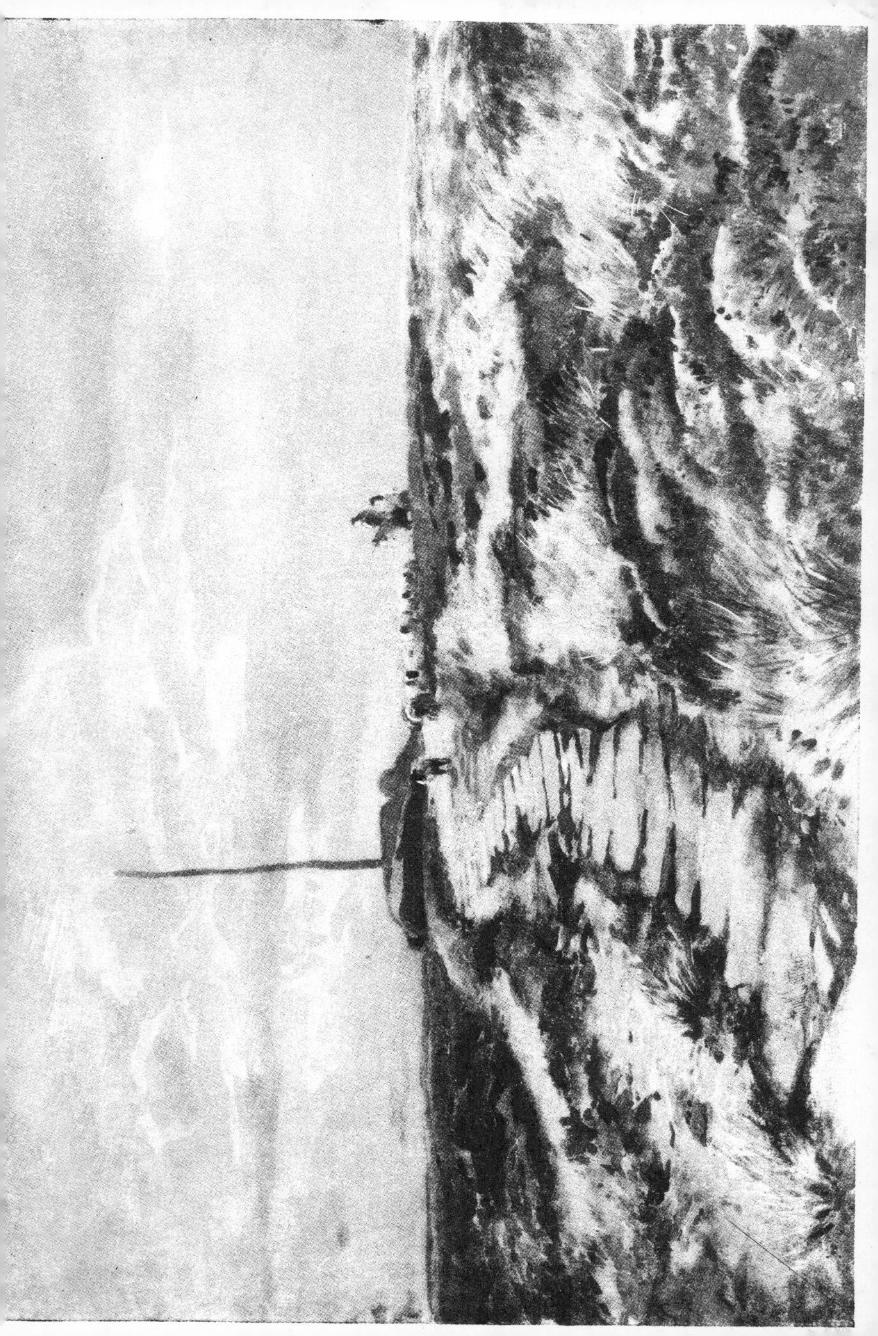

By courtesy of Alasdair Alpin MacGregor

"River Noe near the Packhorse Bridge and Jacob's Ladder, Edale"

FOREWORD

THIS little book does not pretend to be a complete history of the Peak District, which would need a large volume and long years of exhaustive research. It is intended rather to create interest in the past story of our villages and hills, and also to preserve many old tales and traditions that are fast slipping into oblivion.

There is an ancient glamour about the Peakland, which makes it feel remote even today—the grey stone manor-houses and deep lanes draw us back irresistibly to olden days, lanes so ancient that when I walk that way I picture the travellers who have long since passed on the Great Journey. There are peaty tracks above wild crags, from whose giddy height is spread a panorama of romantic beauty: awesome lonesome spots twixt earth and heaven with fantastic rocks shaped like beasts turned to stone as everlasting guardians of their stronghold. So was it when Early Man worshipped the Sun god—Time has not changed the rugged majesty of the High Peak.

It is gratifying to think that after seven years of circulation a fourth edition of my little book is called for.

I hope it will still be helpful to the many visitors and campers who come to explore the Hope Valley and District every year.

Peakland's quiet history is going on today in the Sheepdog Trials, the Village Wakes and other activities of a rural population, whilst farmers are working harder than ever to produce our food, contending with snowstorms and droughts as of old. I send a greeting to them, and to all who love our little corner of Derbyshire.

Grateful thanks are acknowledged to the Derbyshire Archæological Society, the County Library, and many people who have kindly lent me family papers, or recounted old traditions. Also to Alasdair Alpine MacGregor for permission to use some of his photographs.

THE AUTHOR.

Shatton,
November 1955

CONTENTS

ILLUSTRATIONS.

Photographs by Alasdair Alpin MacGregor, A. W. Waterhouse, Mrs. Watling and the author. Line drawings by G. Hull, Ray Dyson, and the author. Maps of Derwent bv J. Bullivant. Other blocks by courtesy by Messrs J. W. Northend Ltd.

I. THIS PEAKLAND

The Kinder Scout Plateau. Remains of Early Man—Tumuli and Earthworks.

OUR Peakland is a land of mountains, so let us begin with High Kinder and the surrounding hills, for without them we should have had no " Peak " story to tell. Our forefathers, with dim ideas of map making and a wholesome dread of personal surveys, just indicated the whole district by a mass of conical molehills scattered thickly and without regard for accuracy. I have before me an old map about 200 years old showing the Peak as an almost unexplored area. There are no roads given, and the few villages are written in as names without connection with each other and rarely in the proper place, whilst the course of the rivers is equally ambiguous. As for the mountains and hills—shall we say they suggest a dream of the Unknown! One strongly suspects the whole thing was copied from Camden's *Britannica*, written in 1586.

These days we discard a peppering of peaks and know Kinder as a high tableland rising in places to 2,000 feet, joined to the backbone of the Pennines, and answering to the name of the Kinder Scout Plateau. The form of it is strangely irregular with long projecting fingers or arms bounded by steep craggy escarpments, and a long tail going backwards to Crookstone Knoll at the eastern or Win Hill end. The middle of the tail is composed of Blackden Edge on the Ashop side, and following round we come in turn to romantic Seal Edge and lofty Fairbrook Naze, which makes a sharp angle. Then by the long barrier of Black Ashop Edge to the promontory of Kinder Scout itself, which juts out at the north-west corner, goes inwards like a bay, and joins the south-western promontory of Kinder Low.

On the south side we have another bay formed by the portion of " coastline " known as Edale Head with Crowden Tor as its eastern " headland." Then comes a narrow clough, wild as a Highland glen, down which the Crowden burn drops in a series of deep pools and waterfalls from the majestic Crowden Tower. A very long irregular promontory composed of Grindslow Knoll and Broadbank Tor takes us round to Grinsdale and a fine amphitheatre of hills, Upper

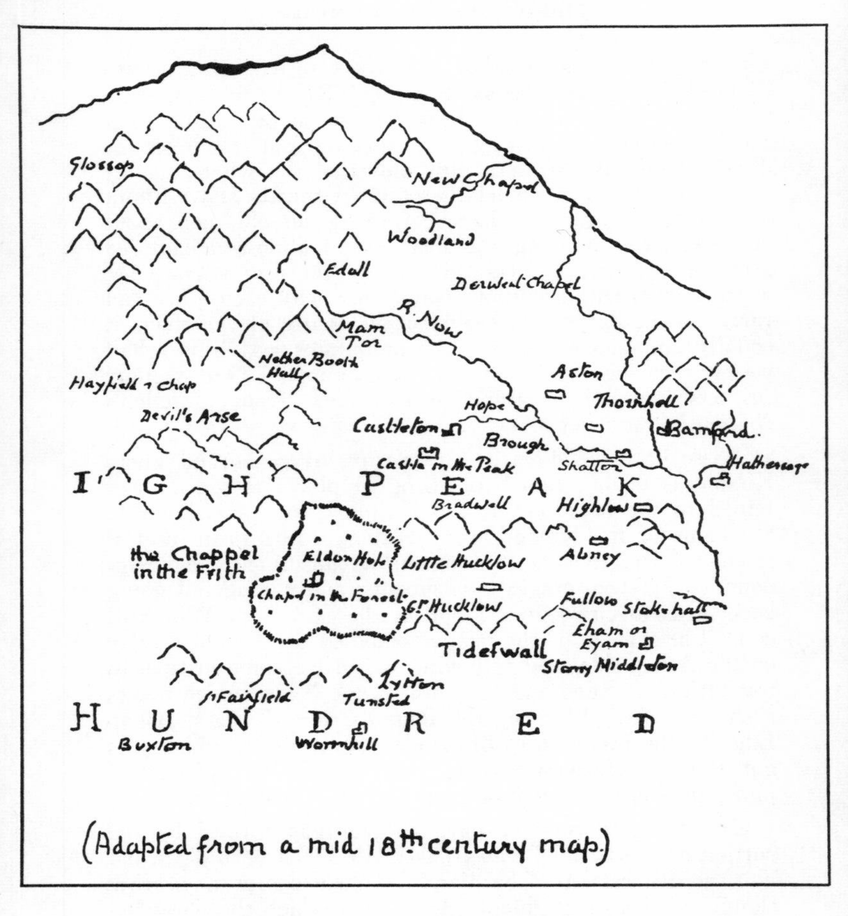

Section of old map of the Peak District

Tor and Nether Tor with Ringing Roger guarding the flank. Thence proceeding east we join the long tail formed by Blackden to our starting-place at Crookstone Knoll.[1] Beyond lies Win Hill looking across the Derwent Valley to the jagged Derwent Edge and Bamford Edge.

This Kinder Tableland forms the backbone of Peakland, and its outline should be understood. The interior of the plateau is largely composed of peat with some dangerous bogs. The whole lump is an important watershed, whose rivulets have carved out deep cloughs scarring the massive sides. Once strictly preserved for grouse, there are certain paths today where one can walk with impunity and see Nature in her wildest mood, but a good map and compass are advisable. It is dangerous to be lost on Kinder.

Long ago these rugged hills formed a last stronghold for successive races of men, where to the last they might defy advancing foes. To us of this generation Kinder is perhaps a last stronghold of Solitude, unspoilt by the work of man. There is no place that can give one the same feeling of utter aloofness from the rest of the world. The long Ashop Valley carrying the Snake Road lies far beneath us to the north. Noedale and Hopedale seem just as remote on the south. Lose Hill, Back Tor and Mam Tor lie across, connected to the Kinder Scout Range by a sweep of high hills along Lord's Seat, and passing the cul de sac pierced by Cowburn Tunnel to Chinley. Beyond Mam Tor lies Castleton and the Limestone part of the district. Here is a very different bit of Peakland with its white cliffs lining deep narrow dales —a land of caverns and underground streams, once a busy centre of the old lead-mining industry.

We have left the Kinder gritstone behind and the shale and sandstone precipice of the Shivery Mountain, as we thread through the limestone dales for a time as far as Stony Middleton. Then making our way to the wide River Derwent, the grey rocks of Millstone Grit appear in a succession of majestic Edges across the valley—Froggat Edge, Burbage Edge and further on Bamford Edge—till we call a halt at the great Ashopton and Derwent Reservoirs. This completes the tour of the part of Peakland with which we

---

[1] The Hope Freeholders had ancient rights of Turbary on Crookstone.

are concerned. Having sketched in the background, the stage is now set for the human side of things—the hamlets that grew into villages, the men and women who lived here long ago, and the churches they built, their early farming efforts and their industries.

As one would expect the hills and moors bear ample evidence of a very early civilisation. There are tumuli marked in plenty on the Ordnance Maps, and doubtless many more await investigation. They cover periods from Neolithic Man to the Saxons, though many have been dispoiled for making and mending stone walls. There were prehistoric burials on the Derwent Moors, round Abney and Offerton and Eyam, Bamford Edge and many other places. More interesting still is the Bronze Age Stone Circle on Wet Withen's Moor near Eyam. Though falling far short of the famous circle of Arborlow, yet it is worth a visit. The stones are lying down, but imagination can picture them rising upright out of the heather towards the sun. A single upright stone once stood in the centre, the diameter of the circle being about 100 feet.

Offerton Moor had another Circle or rather Oval about 85 feet at its greatest length, and containing four middle stones. The surrounding slight bank alone survives, for the stones that once stood on it were carried off bit by bit for gateposts. A small Circle on Abney Moor was mentioned by the great antiquarian Dr. Pegge in 1783 as being in a fair state of preservation, though about twenty years later another antiquarian, Major Rooke, was complaining of its condition. The *Victorian County History* states that thirty years before its publication in 1904 some stones were still standing on the rampart, though Pennington had reported it in 1877 as destroyed to build a wall. These ancient stones must have been very tempting for walls and gateposts. Many Cairns too suffered in like fashion when the moorlands were enclosed. Other small circles were found on Froggatt and Hathersage Moors.

Higgar Tor, that romantic hill crowned with crags above Hathersage, has long been associated with "Druid Worship," but there is no authentic support for this![1] Real History lies just across on Carlwark, which is an ancient British Fortress,

---

[1] **Formerly lots of things were erroneously connected with the Druids.**

and well sited too. The military engineers of past ages selected a rocky platform on the top of a hill about 600 feet long and 200 feet wide, with a vertical drop on three sides. Once the edges of the platform were guarded by a wall of huge stones, which have gradually fallen down the sides and lie around in a tumbled scattered state. On the unprotected side the builders threw up a great rampart of earth about twenty feet thick, faced with mighty stones of natural shape. They knew not the use of mortar so crammed small pebbles in the cavities. This rampart sloped back into the fort to give defenders access to the wall. The only entrance was by a path along the base of the artificial scarp which wound up a narrow walled passage of rude stonework reaching the summit on the south side. Attackers trying to force the gate would come under a hail of missiles from above. One would like to know how the defenders fared in a siege, and who made bold to attack such a stronghold. It is interesting to note that two silver bracelets were unearthed in the vicinity, perhaps the property of some Bronze Age chieftain.

From Carlwark we turn to the numerous defence trenches still plainly visible on many hillsides such as on Win Hill. They must have formed part of a very early plan for holding the security of Peakland summits as last strongholds. A deep trench called Grey Dyke showing between Brough and *Bradwell on the hillside of Shatton has attracted much speculation. It has been assigned to the Romans but is more probably Early British.

The summit of Mam Tor shows a complete camp classed as one of the famous earthworks and occupying about 16 acres. This too has been accredited to the Romans, but the shape is definitely wrong. Roman camps were rectangular. Possibly they made use of it as a lookout, for its date is much older. The so-called Danes Camp on Camp Hill behind Hathersage Church is a high steep-sided mound of unknown origin. A lane cuts through it going up to Moorseats. Evidently it has been used for military purposes and is probably much earlier than the Danes, like the famous Danes Dyke at Flamborough. On the other hand Derbyshire once formed part of Danish Mercia after the Treaty of Wedmore, and much fighting is known to have taken place in the Peak between the inhabitants and the Sea

---

***The wide mound of this entrenchment is thought to give rise to the village name originally spelt BRADWALL (Braodwall).**

Rovers who had come to stay. Odin Mine is said to have been worked by the Danes who named it after a Norse god.

When King Edwin ruled Northumbria fierce struggles took place against the heathen Mercian King Penda, which have yielded finds of spear heads and broken weapons in this neighbourhood. To this period is assigned the traditional battle of Win Hill and Lose Hill, but none can prove the truth of it.

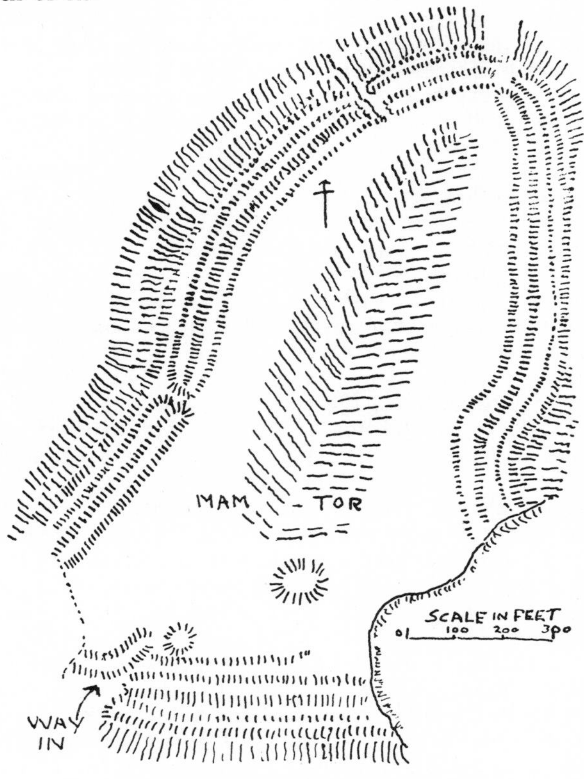

Early British Camp on Mam Tor

The museums of Sheffield, Derby and Buxton show many valuable relics of these distant times taken from Barrows or accidentally found in digging. There are doubtless many more waiting to be unearthed. Farmers have little time today for noting small objects revealed by tractor ploughing, but finds have turned up now and then most unexpectedly. A farmer's son picked up a long smooth flint implement on the verge of Shatton Moor above Bradwell which he took for an old spear head. It is seven inches long and weighs 17 oz. The end is slightly chisel-shaped and sharpened to a fair cutting edge. Had it been a cutting tool and not a weapon at all? Expert opinion would be useful here.

And so with the local finding of a flint we end the first chapter of this short story of The Peak.

II. THE ROMANS AT BROUGH

ALONG the main road from Hathersage and Bamford to Hope one passes an inn called the Traveller's Rest. Opposite this stands Brough Mill and a substantial bridge leading to the picturesque little hamlet on the by-road to Bradwell Dale. It is a local bus stop where a few people alight and go down the gentle hill towards the grey stone cottages. Strangers may pause on the bridge and gaze over the parapet into the water, thinking perhaps that a cornmill in such a setting has romance. Two old wooden water-wheels still turn with a pleasing rumble to grind corn and meal, just as they have done for centuries. Yes it is old, very old, for a mill stood here in the twelfth century,[1] though the present building only dates from 1924 following a disastrous fire. Through an open doorway one catches a glimpse of white mealy sacks and a youth in dusty overalls.

But that is not all in this wayside hamlet. For instance, why is it called Brough? The answer lies across in the green meadow behind the mill where the Roman fort of Anavio lies buried. This formed part of the defences of northern Britain nearly 2,000 years ago. In 1904 it was partly excavated, yielding enough information to give it a definite place in history. A strongly walled rectangle 336 ft. × 275 ft. with evidence of four gateways was discovered. The base of a small tower stood in the south-west corner, whilst in the southern portion of the enclosure the Praetorium or Headquarters buildings revealed their foundations. The northern half may show the position of the soldiers' long huts, which were sometimes of stone in a permanent fort, though often in wood. On the site of the Praetorium a small underground chamber aroused much speculation. It was thought to have been a strongroom for Standards and other valuables in time of danger. Later it was probably used as a well, suggested by the remains of an ancient tub or wooden bucket found therein. Stone steps had been added after construction perhaps to replace a former wooden ladder. The last stage of use was obviously for rubbish, because many broken stones, smashed pottery, bones, grindstones and small

---

[1] Mentioned in the Pipe Rolls of King John's time and belonged to Philip de Strelley.

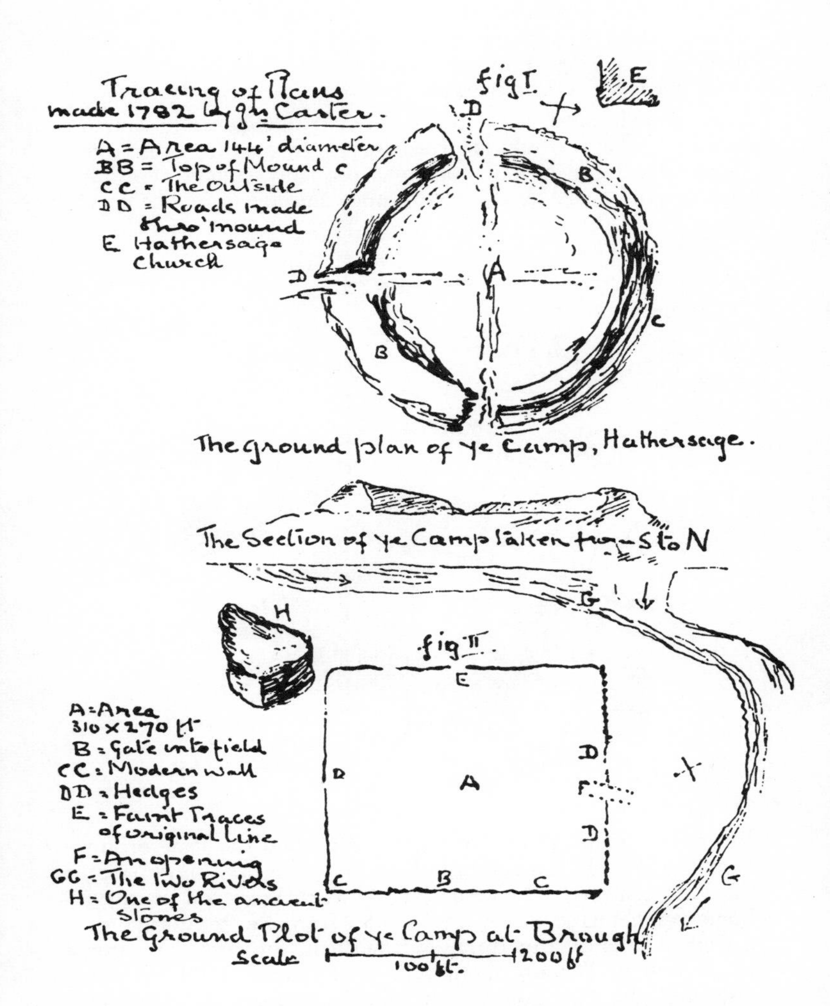

Old plans of Camp Hill, Hathersage, and Roman Fort at Brough

gritstone balls for catapult missiles were lying about at the bottom. And of course some tell-tale coins were amongst the debris—Roman soldiers always seemed careless with their money, scattering it around just where succeeding generations needed it as confirmation of a date of occupation!

At Anavio most of the coins were small, suggesting fourth century, which would be the time of departure from the fort. One large bronze coin was probably second century, also a gold-piece of Augustus and another large coin of

Vespasian (about A.D. 71) were found around the Praetorium outside the well. In spite of these finds the first building of the Fort can only be placed roughly as early second century. Some further clue to the date comes from the tombstone of a Roman who died in Italy, and had held the post of Censor to Anavio in Britain about A.D. 105. Incidentally he was doubtless the first government official to make a census in the Hope Valley! The brief inscription proves that Rome knew our early inhabitants as the "Anavionensian Britons." They scheduled the River Noe as the River Anava, and stated on a Roman milestone found in Buxton that Anavio was ten miles distant along the road they constructed.

This interesting historic road can still be traced in part. The old writers Camden and Jones called it Bathgate, but in 1767 it appears as *Bathumgate, the name it bears today. John Jones in 1572 speaks of it as "an highway forced across

Excavations of Fort Walls, Brough

the moores, all paved of such antiquity as none can express, called Bathgate." From Buxton it ran through Fairfield going north-east for two miles, then turning north-north-east made straight for Brough via Peak Forest, present railway station (now obliterated by quarries), across the Tideswell and Bradwell Moors to Smalldale at the corner of Bradwell, thence it coincides with the present Streetfield Road to Brough. Note the name Streetfield, and the story behind it.

---

*Now spelt Bathamgate.

Aquis was the Roman name for Buxton, and they knew and used the healing waters. A military road connected with Little Chester Fort just outside Derby, and at Brough came an important junction linking up with Templeborough near Rotherham, and a position known during the last two centuries as Melandra near Glossop. We shall consider these roads later.

Anavio was a natural stronghold at the meeting of the Noe with Bradwell Brook. On the north side the land fell steeply to the river. Moreover it commanded a fine wide view of all the surrounding country. When catapults mounted on the corner turrets were the heaviest artillery there was no object in seeking a dominating hilltop for a site. A good all-round view was more necessary, whilst the running water provided natural means for bathing. Remains of a large bath-house for the soldiers with colonnades were found near the Mill. The icy winter waters from the high hills and Peak Cavern may even have been warmed by a hypocaust system. The Romans never did things by halves, and their civilisation was up to our own in most ways.

Who were these men who watched the Hope Valley long ago? The answer to that question was ascertained by the finding of a most interesting inscribed stone, in broken pieces, during the excavation of the underground chamber in the Praetorium. After much trouble the lettering was deciphered and reads thus: "In honour of the Emperor Titus Aelius Hadrianus Antoninus Augustus Pius, Father of his country (erected by) the First Cohort of Aquitanians, under Julius Verus, governor of Britain, and under the direct orders of Capitonius Fuscius, praefect of the cohort."

The cohort were not legionaries but auxiliary troops, who were used to man these smaller border forts under Roman officers. It is thought the stone may refer to the rebuilding or strengthening of Anavio at the time of unrest and revolt among the fierce tribes of Brigantes about A.D. 158. The north had not adopted the Roman way of life like the south, and the occupation of these desolate parts of upper Britain was purely military. A sullen submissiveness would characterise the natives of the High Peak, with some local barter from those dwelling near the fort. The working of leadmines around Bradwell and Castleton might have been enforced on the inhabitants, though there are traditions

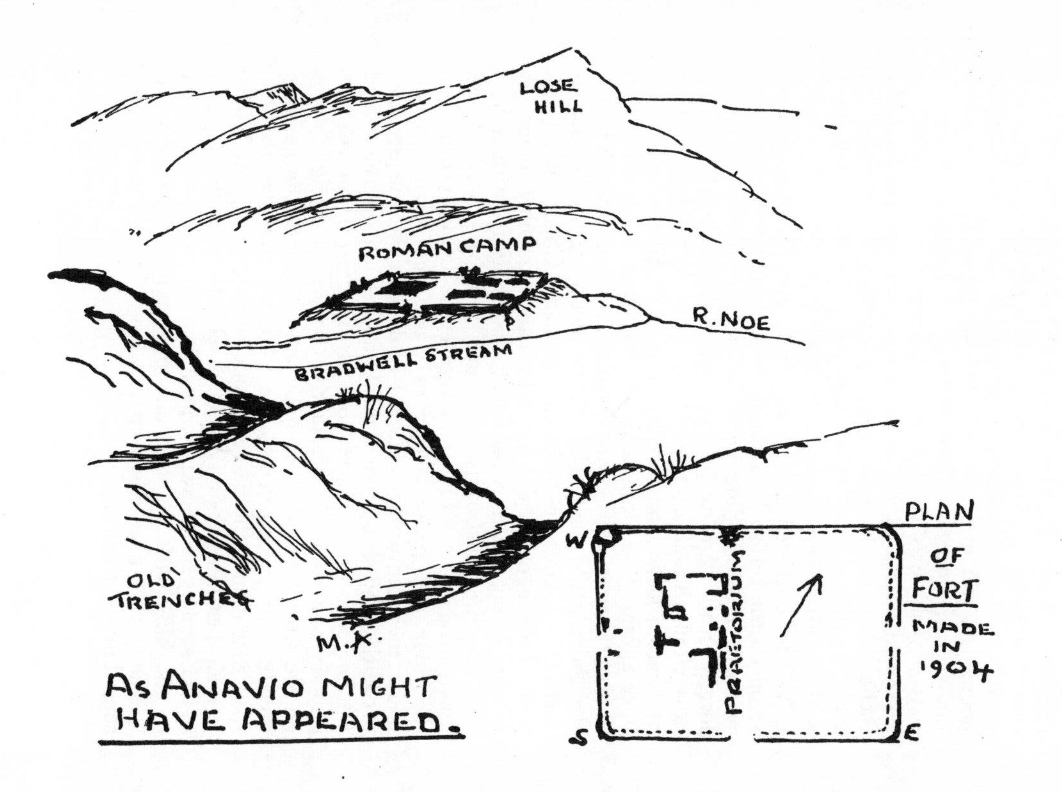
LOSE HILL
ROMAN CAMP
R. NOE
BRADWELL STREAM
OLD TRENCHES
M.X.
PLAN OF FORT MADE IN 1904
PRAETORIUM
W
S
E
As ANAVIO MIGHT HAVE APPEARED.

of slaves being sent from France and Italy to work in a settlement under Roman officials, and this practice was common in the empire. The near presence of the soldiers would prevent trouble breaking out among the poor wretches doomed to toil underground. We do know the mines were known and worked in Roman times, and one of the famous pigs of lead was found when digging the foundations of Bradwell school in 1874. It was twenty inches long, five inches wide and three inches high. Other Roman lead pigs were found around Matlock and bore the name of the region Lutadarum—one was dated in Hadrian's reign.

We have drifted a long way back into the past since we stood on the bridge by Brough Mill with the rumble of the water wheels mingling with the occasional noise of heavy lorries on the high road a hundred or so yards away. Let us now climb the hill by the old cart road to the lower corner of Shatton Edge, and here try to picture Anavio as it would have appeared to a couple of Britons about 1,750 years ago Today the grey Derbyshire sheep are grazing peacefully over the short green turf which once again buries the ancient fort. They know nothing of the First Cohort who lived there long ago. Only the hills can remember when the trumpets rang out to rouse sleepy auxiliaries from their huts The morning mist rolls away and the day's bustle begins down in the lines. Our two keen-eyed Britons creep along the ridge and pause awhile to watch the soldiers muster under their centurions. Hatred rankles in their hearts, then presently they slip down the hill to seek an interview with the praefect on a matter of buying corn from the fort granary and to study afresh the chances of a night attack on the strong walls. Nominally at peace with the garrison they have often seen the Roman soldiers march over the steep road that climbs the mountainside to the north, but Kinder is their fastness—their sacred homeland—and the tramp of nailed sandals on paving-stones is hateful to their ears. Sons of the hills with the freedom of Peakland in their souls Perhaps as we gaze down on this long-lost fort, we too feel something of their spirit.

III. THE ROYAL FOREST OF THE PEAK

THE Forest of the Peak was a wild district forming part of the inheritance of the Anglo-Saxon kings, and was already royal property at the time of Domesday. Large tracts of it were included in the Parish of Hope. One must not think of it as all timber, because in olden times the word forest embraced mountain, heath and bogland, where wolves, deer and wild boars roamed at will. When primitive cultivation was possible small hamlets occurred here and there owned by Saxon thanes and socmen. Such was Peak Forest when William the Conqueror handed it over to his natural son, William Peverel, in 1068. The Peverel family held it for less than 100 years, for in 1155 a younger Peverel was disinherited for poisoning the Earl of Chester, and his land forfeited to the Crown. In 1372 it passed to the Duchy of Lancaster.

At the beginning of the twelfth century the Forest included the whole of north-west Derbyshire, and was divided into three districts known as Campagna (open country), Hopedale and Longendale. The latter included all the district round Glossop, whilst the Campagna was situated around Chapel-en-le-Frith area on the south and south-west, Hopedale stretched as far as Stoke and Tideswell, and contained the seven " berewicks " of Aston, Edale, half of Offerton, Shatton, Stoke and Tideswell. In the Forest Pleas held in 1286 the Boundaries were carefully defined. They make an interesting study to those who know their Peakland, and I will give the quotation from the *Victoria County History, Vol. I,* in its original quaint wording:

" The metes and bounds of the Forest of the Peak begin on the south at the new place of Goyt, and thence by the River Goyt as far as the River Etherow; and so by the River Ethrow to Longley Croft at Longdendale; thence by a certain footpath to the head of Derwent; and from the head of Derwent to a place called Mythomstede Bridge, and from Mythom Bridge to the River Bradwell; and from

---

[1] The name appears as " Mittenforde " in the 1274 Inquisition, and it is unlikely a bridge then existed. Mythomstede Bridge would be a later name used by the translators of the Latin document about 1820.

the River Bradwell as far as a certain place called Hucklow; and from Hucklow to the Great Dell of Hazelbache; and from that dell as far as Little Hucklow; and from Little Hucklow to the brook of Tideswell, and so to the River Wye, and to the new place of Goyt."

The area did not quite coincide with the Hundred of the High Peak, and the ancient boundaries remained until the seventeenth century. Each of the three divisions had its own set of Forest officials under the Chief Bailiff, who lived at Peak Castle. The dungeons were used for the worst law-breakers, and the Baillie for impounding sheep and cattle found feeding illegally on preserved land. No actual Court of Justice seems to have been held there. The seat of administration was in the centre of the Forest equidistant from Castleton, Tideswell and Bowden. Here stood a Forest Hall, known as "The Chamber," with a chapel attached. Later, about 1225, the chapel was removed to Bowden, which henceforth became known as Chapel-en-le-Frith. Courts were sometimes held at Tideswell, which was a place of some importance. These Forest Courts were known as "Eyres," and often considerable time elapsed between their sittings, but smaller local courts were held known as "Swain-moots" and "Attachment Courts," to deal with smaller cases, and to decide what law-breakers must be detained or allowed on bail until the Great Court met. It is interesting to note that the great majority of "deer stealers" came from the upper class of society, and included prominent members of the nobility! In fact it seems to have been the fashionable thing in Feudal times to poach the King's game from Peak Forest, and the fines formed an important item of revenue. Venison trespass records of the thirteenth century include William de Ferrers, Earl of Derby (who died before coming to justice), Ralph de Beaufoy of Trusley, Richard Curzon, Henry de Elton, and William May the Earl's huntsman, for having taken 1,000 deer during the six years when Earl Derby was Chief Bailiff (1216-1222). Three of them were imprisoned but afterwards released with heavy fines.

Other members of the nobility and gentry convicted for the fun of poaching were the Earl of Arundel, Sir Thomas Furnival, lord of Sheffield, Matthew de Hathersage, one of the Bagshawes,[1] and I regret to say some members of the church, including the Rector of Manchester and the Vicar of Sheffield! Matthew de Hathersage was charged with having "a Buckstall in his great wood at Hathersage barely two bowshots from the King's Forest," and he had to pay 20 marks. The Buckstall was a kind of extended netted trap for catching deer. It would seem that Robin Hood and Little John were not the only poachers in the district, and some of the local tradition centring round their magic names may have origin elsewhere.

Convictions of humble men are rarely recorded. Doubtless they were severely punished in the cruel Norman times, and the hand of justice may have acted quickly without reference to the Great Court. Possibly Peak Castle could tell some grim stories if its walls could speak. On the other hand it is good to note that in later times certain poor men were pardoned by the King's Mercy, when brought to the "Eyre" for deer stealing.

A word now about the various ranks of Forest officials who acted under the Chief Bailiff. First in rank came the Verderers, who were elected by Freeholders in the County on a writ addressed to the Sheriff. They were men of some position, who held duty for life, and sometimes the office was hereditary. They presided over small courts with power to try minor offences. Their badge of office was an axe. Next in rank came the Foresters, also men of some standing locally, who were responsible for "attaching" offenders, which might be done in three different ways (1) By goods and chattels; (2) By pledges and mainprize; (3) By his body (meaning of course imprisonment). The offender could go on bail if he produced two pledges, the number increasing for further crimes until at the fourth he was carried off to durance vile in the Castle. If the poacher was caught red-handed, however, with a slain deer in his possession or blood on his clothes, it was prison at once for him without any chance of bail!

In Edward I or III time a Riding Forester was appointed over the others, receiving the high salary for those days of 12 pence a day. The Peak had the famous Eyre family amongst its hereditary Foresters, who held land in Hopedale

---

[1] **The Bagshawes of Ford Hall are an ancient Peakland family.**

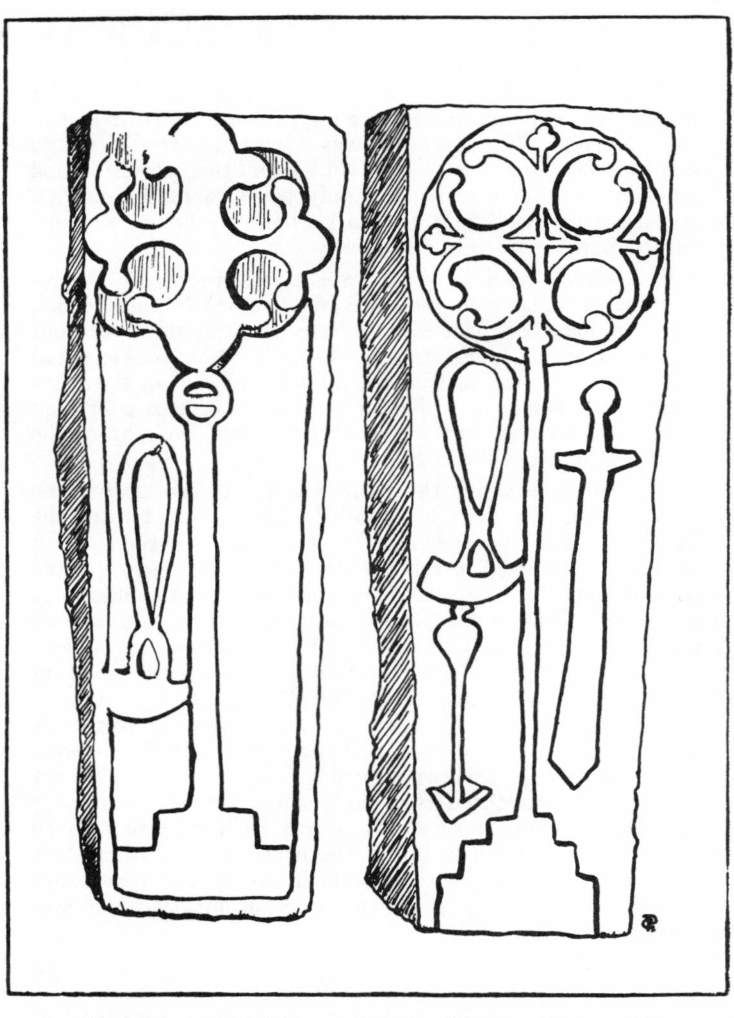

13th Century Tombstones of Forest Officials to be seen in Hope Church

—By courtesy of Mrs. Watling and J. W. Northend, Ltd.

in return for discharging obligations, which included attending all courts in person. It was considered an honourable appointment. After them came the Agisters and Woodwards. The former were chiefly concerned with cattle and sheep grazing rights, and the collection of dues from those who were allowed to use specified parts of the Forest for the purpose. Woe betide those who let their flocks and herds stray on forbidden ground! There are gruesome records of 300 sheep with their lambs being impounded in Peak Castle yard to starve to death without food or water.

Woodwards were employed by owners of manors adjacent to the Forest or sometimes actually within its bounds, where the King's game had full rights. Their duties were to guard against trespass and they had power to "attach" criminals. A Hatchet was their symbol of office. The old Hope name of Woodruffe is derived from the Woodwards or Wood Reeves. Towards the end of the fourteenth century one hears also of Rangers, who had to ensure the Forest Law was properly kept. In addition to all these officials there were Wolf Keepers, traditionally associated with Wormhill. They became so renowned as trappers that Henry II paid for two of them to cross to his domains in Normandy and deal with the wolves over there. The beasts seem to have been plentiful and ferocious in Peak Forest all through the feudal days, and some lingered up to the time of Henry VII in their remote northern fastness. There were two payments made in connection with wolves between 1160 and 1161. During the thirteenth century a colt was strangled by a wolf in Edale and in 1255 two sheep are mentioned in the accounts of Gervase de Bernake also killed by these savage animals. Wolf traps were set throughout the Forest twice a year and the vast domains beaten from end to end to keep down the dangerous pest. Several place-names bear the word wolf in the district, such as Wolf Pit and Wolf Stone.

Another menace to life in the great Forest was the wild charging of the deer, who trampled men and dogs to death. With such an enormous population of royal game, it is not surprising the local inhabitants wished to keep them down by illicit slaying! Corn was trampled and fences broken, so that agriculture suffered badly from the incursions of these fierce and pampered animals protected by harsh laws. Whatever else starved the deer must be fed and fattened on the land. In later times, however, the farmers encroached with their peaceful cattle more and more, in spite of fines, and the deer in turn grew hungry. Things were coming to a pass between agricultural needs and the Chase, when the inhabitants of the district "being desirous to be freed from the severity of the Forest Laws and Customs, and the incommodiousness of deer lying and feeding in their corn and grass, and other inconveniences," petitioned Charles I to end the state of affairs. This was about 1640, but unfortunately the King had other troubles at the moment. The Civil War came, and beyond making a survey of the Forest nothing was done until the year 1674, when Disafforrestation took place (I hope I have used the correct word!), and the deer were all rounded up and killed.

During the Survey a map had been made showing all the area in different colouring, and the old Forest Wall. And so ended long centuries of tyranny and hardship. In future men could plough up land without fear of fines or imprisonment, and their flocks and herds could wander in pastures new. The wolves had gone—and now the deer, but many may have hankered in secret for a stolen haunch of venison!

Photograph by courtesy of A. F. Waterhouse

INTERIOR OF HOPE CHURCH.

—*By courtesy of Mrs. Watling and Messrs. Northend, Ltd.*

OLD SAXON CROSS, HOPE

IV. THE ANCIENT PARISH OF HOPE

IN discussing the great Forest of the Peak, we have seen that Hope was a prominent place in Feudal Times. It was in fact one of the largest parishes in England, dating from Saxon days, extending to the Woodlands on the north, nearly to Buxton on the south; to Stoke and Nether Padley on the east, also taking in the present Parish of Bradwell, both the Hucklows, Wardlow and Foolow, and in early times Tideswell. On the west it stretched towards Chapel-en-le-Frith and joined Glossop Parish on the north west.

At the Domesday Survey in 1088 the Manor was returned as containing seven "Berewicks," comprising—"Aidele (Edale), Estune (Aston), Scetune (Shatton), half of Uffertune (Offerton), Tideswelle, Storche (Stoke) and Muchedreswell (?). King Edward had ten Caracutes of land to the geld. There was a mill rendering 5/4, 30 acres of meadow, woodland for pannage (grazing) in places; there were 30 villeins and four bordars having six ploughs, and most important of all—a church and a priest. So that Hope church goes back before the Norman conquest, the oldest authentic place of worship in this part of the Peak.

A Saxon Cross without arms stands in the Churchyard in spite of certain wanderings. It was discovered when the old School House was demolished in 1858, part of it being used as a door lintel, and the other part built into the walls. Later it was in the vicarage garden, but now stands near the south porch of the church. The arms may have been broken off in Puritan times, when in 1643 all crosses in open places were to be removed and destroyed. The six-sided steps in the churchyard may or may not have formed the base. More probably they belonged to another market cross. The date, judging from the style of carved decoration has been given as probable ninth century, *County History of Derbyshire,* though some writers have thought it belonged to an earlier period of Saxon missionary zeal in the north west of England when these Christian symbols were set up as rallying points before the erection of churches. Comparison with the crosses at Eyam and Bakewell is of interest.

The present Hope Church probably occupies the same site as the Saxon building. It dates from the thirteenth century, though mainly fourteenth and fifteenth century. The tower and spire are fourteenth century with part of the outer walls, also the arches and columns of the Nave and south doorway. The South Porch and Parvise over it (a small chamber), windows, clerestry and low-pitched battlemented roof are fifteenth century. Two ancient tomb slabs bearing Early English crosses were found under the foundation wall when the old Chancel was pulled down. The other carving on them depicts forestry implements, and suggests the grave of two officials of Peak Forest residing in Hopedale. They are described as thirteenth century. (See page 22).

In 1882 the Chancel was entirely rebuilt, and the East End in 1908, when the stone Screen was erected. There is some interesting old wood carving on the pulpit. Alterations were made to the porch in 1882. In the Chancel a small brass may be seen to Henry Balguy, who died March, 1685, and also a brass to the Woodroofes. This old family died out in Hope about the middle of last century, perpetuating the name in the Woodroofe Arms Inn. At one time they supplied successions of Church Wardens and Parish Clerks, whose careful accounts have preserved many interesting facts about former Hope doings.

Country life centred round the old Parish Churches, which represented much more than mere places of worship on a Sunday. It is to the old Registers and Archives we go for general information about the people—their lands and possessions, their joys and sorrows. The church was a rallying point in common danger, a sanctuary for fugitives, a home for guidance and comfort, and a last Resting Place.

We can obtain a fair picture of current conditions in any period that has been faithfully recorded, not only of the people's daily lives, but also their reactions to the larger affairs of state that touched their quiet backwater. The late Dr. Porter, one of Sheffield's leading physicians, retired to Hope and made exhaustive researches into the history of the ancient parish. His book now out of print, has been of great help and interest to me in the compiling of this chapter, together with the loan of two valuable illustrations. These records deal mainly with the period dating from Queen Elizabeth, though there are a few gleanings from earlier times. Mention has already been made of the various forest officers dwelling in Hope, the chief of whom was William de Eyr in the reign of Henry III. He seems to have been the "father" of the great Peakland clan bearing the name of Eyre, which will be discussed later on when dealing with old Manor Houses.

In Edward I reign a castle at Hope is mentioned, but whether this referred to Castleton or the old trenched mounds in a field behind the Woodroofe Arms, or to the ruins of the Roman Fort at Brough about half a mile away, one cannot say. It is quite possible part of the thick walls were still standing at that time, and the name Brough or Burgh is clearly derived from the fort.

The Manor of Hope had been given by Henry II to his son John, who disposed of the Ecclesiastical Rights in 1192 to Hugo de Novant, Bishop of Coventry and Lichfield. Tideswell became a separate parish in 1254, and its beautiful church rose to eclipse the parent building, and to earn the proud title of Cathedral of the Peak.

The villages and hamlets comprising Hope Parish formerly were as follows, taken from the Church Wardens Accounts for 1661—Hope, Bradwell, Thornhill, Aston, Brough, Shattons, Offerton, Woodlands, Highloe, Stoak Nether Padley, Abney and Grange, Great Hucklow, Little Hucklow, Grindlow, Wardlow, Hazelbadge, Shawcross and Fearnylee. A penny rate was levied. Extracts from the Accounts dated 1686-7 include some curious items, such as:—

	£	s.	d.
"Paid to the Ringers the 29th of May ...		5	0
Paid to the Ringers the 5th of November...		5	0
Paid for tenn foxes and their heads... ...	3	16	8
Paid for five fox cubs	1	1	8
Paid for seven Boson heads (Badgers) ...		7	0
Paid for 25 Raven heads		8	4
Paid for 205 Urchin heads	1	14	2

(The last item sounds alarming, but merely referred to humble hedgehogs!)

In 1688 3/6 was paid "for a book of prayers for a Day of Thanks giving for ye Prince of Wales" (Son of James II and afterwards known as The Old Pretender). Hope went strong for the Stuarts. In 1689 are two very curious entries worth quoting in full:—

	s.	d.
"Paid for 5 calves . . . to leather ye Bells.	1	8
For a Board to stop a drop on ye leads above mr. bagshaw's seat	1	0"

Early in the next century we find Bamford Singers were paid 2/6 and Castleton Singers 3/-, who evidently sang better! A new Weather Cock was also bought or made costing £2 15s. followed by an item—" for sett ye Cock up 2/6." In July, 1730, the church was reseated, and in 1733 new bells were weighed and tuned at Bawtry requiring the keep of two men and two horses for four days over the business. Raven heads and foxes still appear periodically and 3/- was paid for catching three Otters in 1739, and on the same line 3/- "for mending ye clock." Ecclesiastical Accounts truly covered a multitude of things!

A basson and hautboys were introduced to help the singing in the year 1759, the innovation requiring a Parish meeting, who granted 16/6 towards the cost. I should love to have heard that choir the following Christmas morning sounding forth the dear old hymns and carols. A few years later one William Jeffrey was paid £1 6s. for playing the basson, and a Bass Viol was purchased in 1769.

If an American happens to see this book, he will be shocked to find that Hope Ringers received 2/- " when New York was taken"! (1776-7). But we must really leave these intriguing old Account Books, and turn to a list of landowners in the Parish in Queen Bess's reign dated 1570. They are a link in local history—staunch supporters of the Mother Church, who often lived some distance away in isolated hamlets, farming their land and taking an interest in Parish concerns. Here are their names and hamlets:—Christopher Eyre of Highlow, knight; Thomas Eyre of Hope, gent; Edmund Woodroofe of Hucklow, gent; William Poynton of Hucklow, yeoman; Robert Glossop of Offerton, gent; George Eyre of Abney, gent; John Downes of Lane Head, yeoman; John Marshall of Bradwall, yeoman; William Cocke of Bradwell, yeoman; Nicholas Thornhill of Thornhill, yeoman; John Trickett of Hope, yeoman; Nicholas Woodwoofe of Hope, gent; William Smythe of Aston, yeoman. The yeoman were the backbone of England, carrying on old traditions, and a sturdy stock.

The Easter Roll for the Parish of Hope in the year 1658 is also of great interest, showing who lived in all the hamlets three hundred years ago. Many old names still survive, Middletons, Halls, Robinsons, Chapmans, Frosts, Marshalls, and so on.

Hope district had sent its quota to prepare for the Spanish Armada. Their names were Thomas Slake, Ralphe Glover, Richard Slake, Edward Halle, Thurstan Halle, Renolde Pursglove, Richard Needham, Robte Arnefeelde, Gilbarte Marshall, Robte Marshall of Thornhill. Between them they provided the following equipment, iii Calivers, iii Arquebuses, ii corselets, ii bills (a staff weapon furnished with spikes at the top and back, with a head like a billhook). The Home Guards of Hope must be proud of these doughty ancestors. In fact we have a lot to be proud of in our ancient Parish.

There seems one bone of contention however—Edale being in the Ecclesiastical Jurisdiction of Castleton since the Reformation does not believe its name appears in the Domesday Survey as a " berewick " of the great Manor of Hope. Yet there it stands for all who will take the trouble to examine the long Manorial Roll, which the *Victoria County History of Derbyshire* gives in full detail. It certainly became associated with Castleton at an early date, but the very word Castleton was unknown in 1088, as the new Norman castle was too young to give rise to the present name of the village. Domesday only tells posterity that Gerneberne and Hundine held the land of William Pevrell's castle in Pechefere (Peak Forest). Returning to the Hope Easter Roll of parishioners, the old Tythe Customs are of interest. There were personal tithes usually 2d. for each person over 16, and ½d. for children or servants, and special Easter dues paid upon livestock. Thus in Hope each cow cost the owner 2d., each calf 1d., sheep grazing was 2d., while each beekeeper paid 2d. for his hives. " Plough Alms " were also given for every plough land. It was a nice old custom binding church and farm together. Moreover a study of the list reveals the farm animals possessed by every farmer in the big scattered parish on Easter Day, 1658. For instance in Brough and Shatton, Anthony Robinson had plough land, two cows and two calves, and Anthony Wood had two cows, two calves, bee hives and sheep, etc. Church Records are a vertible goldmine to the keen antiquarian.

Hope Vicarage seems to have been endowed between 1224-38. No surname appears for William the first vicar. There have been thirty-three vicars since the earliest record, and the list contains a Bagshaw and two Eyres. The second one,

Edmund Eyre, 1602, was buried "the XV April without service or bell in ye night," and seems to have been a bad lad! Another interesting padre in 1650 was Thos. Bocking, of whom the Parliamentary Commissioners spoke as "the present Incumbent, formerly in arms against the Parliament, and reputed scandalous"! All honour to the Royalist Fighting Parson, who took up arms for his King. His name is carved on the pulpit door, where he is described as a teacher in the old Free School founded in Tudor times. It was a native of Thornhill hamlet who left £100 to provide for a resident schoolmaster to come and live in Hope, on condition the parishioners would build a school house. The messuage was bought in 1632, and trustees appointed. They were Thos. Eyre of Highlow, Esq., Elize Woodroofe of Hope, Esq., Thos. Balguy of Aston (gent), Wm. Leadbeater (clerk), Richard Stevenson of Over Shatton (gent), Thos. Eyre of Nether Shatton (gent), Thos. How of Little Ashop (gent), Robert Ward of Twitchill, Adam Eyre of Crookhill, Wm. Glossop of Offerton, Francis Wilcockson of Abney, Nicholas Hadfield of Hope, Richard Middleton and Godfrey Kirke of Bradwall, (aforesaid yeomen).

The village of Hope itself with its quiet grey stone houses clustered about the old church, the stocks forming the gateway, the peaceful cawing of rooks in the big trees, and the busy smithies by the roadside suggests an incongruity with the bustle of modern traffic going through its midst. To me, it is always dreaming quietly of a long past and a place in history.

Even the Post Office, once an Inn, The Durham Ox, is 400 years old, whilst the Old Hall Inn was once a manor house. Along Edale Road we find the romantic Higher Hall with its reputed secret passage to the church, when it was a priests' house. The neat cottages are centuries old, and once busy hives of weaving and spinning and homely industries; for Hope people in olden times made their own occupational trade, without going forth to work in other places. The old mill down by the picturesque bridge and weir all have a charm and quiet dignity in keeping with the capital of Hopedale and the home of our Mother Church.

V. ANCIENT ROADS AND BRIDLEWAYS

Roman roads, Packhorse travel, Old Bridges and Fords, Flooded Rivers and Crossings Perilous.

IT is thought that the large animals dwelling in Britain after the Ice Age, made a definite trail through Peakland from Yorkshire to reach the salt in Cheshire. If so they were the oldest road-makers in these parts. Early men of the Neolithic and Bronze Ages certainly made tracks over the hills, some of which later developed into packhorse trails. They chose the hilly routes to avoid the swamps and dense undergrowth in the valleys. Some of these ways may have been used by the Romans before they engineered their own roads.

We have already noted the famous Bathgate or Bathamgate, as it is now called, and you will remember there was a junction near the Fort of Anavio (Brough). The branch leading to Templeborough may be seen on the Hallam Moors beyond Stanedge as the Long Causeway, where the paving stones have escaped destruction. Their constant use by pack animals right up to the eighteenth century has prevented them from being overgrown by moss and heather. This road is interesting to compare with Wade's Road over the Whitby Moors, some of which still remains with the drainage ditches on either side.

The Long Causeway Road is supposed to have gained Stannage via Bamford, using a ford over the Derwent. Whether the steep straight lane up Bamford Clough had anything to do with it one cannot say. Popular local belief clings to Saltergate and the paved winding lane up Hurst Clough. But then many sunk lanes were paved by single flags in the middle for packhorse traffic of the seventeenth and eighteenth centuries, and the finding of such paving stones laid in single file is no proof whatsoever of the Romans. Parts of the Long Causeway may have been repaired from time to time, though many stones are deeply grooved by the hoofs of centuries. Long before Sheffield was thought of, the old road kept to the high ground along Lidgate dropping down into the Don Valley to Templeborough, another fort in the Roman defence chain.

The link from Anavio with the fort near Glossop followed the River Noe for a short way, then slanted up the steep hillside where Win Hill merges with the lower Kinder slopes and crossed the high barrier separating Noedale from the Ashop Valley. Using the fairly easy descent near Blackley Hey, it forded the Ashop River near its junction with the Alport stream and reached Melandra by Lady Clough along " Doctor's Gate." I have never found an explanation for the word " Doctor," and conclude it is a corruption of some older name. It has been connected with Dr. Faust and the Devil!

Yet another Roman road is thought to have connected Anavio with Bakewell, and possibly Chesterfield. This went over Shatton and Abney Moors, passing near Eyam and Stoney Middleton, where coins have been found. An old bath used to be shown at the latter place by St. Martin's well. Is it possible these old stone and cement plunge-baths beside chalybeate springs were in former times used by miners to cleanse lead from their bodies? There is another one beneath a roofless shed in a field near Eccles Lane, Bradwell, close to the ancient house called Eden Tree, or Edwin's Tree as it was once known. Both of these old baths exist near lead mining, and where springs of warmish water occur, similar to the well-known waters of Buxton.[1]

After the final departure of the Romans their roads must have been used by the Britons and later by the Saxon conquerors. Very likely they used some of the stone for building purposes, as they also used the walls of the fort. To this day farmers have utilised the stones of Anavio, and one may see the broken column of a Roman pillar built into a gatepost at Brough.[2] It would need a tremendous exploration to uncover all the old routes, which might have sunk many feet in softer ground. Occasionally Roman coins have turned up. One was found at Thornhill years ago.

By the time of the Domesday Survey many other lanes must have existed connecting Saxon hamlets and farmsteads. There would be tracks through the great Forest of the Peak for the use of officials and the keeping of forest boundaries.

---

[1] They were used by persons suffering from skin troubles for centuries.

[2] This was in situ 1782. See sketch copied from original drawing.

Many old crosses were set up as landmarks along ancient routes, which have created much Antiquarian argument. Were they originally parish boundaries, forest partitions or wayside praying crosses set up by the monks for travellers? One may be found at Edale Head on the old packhorse road to Hayfield, called The Monk's road. Others stood once on Rushup Edge (Swyer Cross referred to in a deed of 1657), and one at Sparrowpit, shown on a plan dated 1712.

Base of Roman Column built into wall tops at Brough copied from sketch made in 1783. Still in its place today.

Another curious upright stone once marked some point on the bleak Offerton Moor, whilst Hope Cross high up on the track over the hills from Hope to Allport is much older than the date it bears. The lettering on its four sides says—"Hope - Sheffield - Glossop - Edale" and the date 1737, carved for the guidance of wayfarers in the packhorse days of travel. Mention should be made of the date on Edale Cross, 1810, and the letters "I.G." It seems that the old cross probably dating from the Cistercian Monks in the twelfth century when they received lands from Henry II around Glossop, had fallen down, and was restored to its Longendale portion of the Royal Forest of the Peak, which proper position by one John Gee of Ashes Farm, Kinder. It was also the old boundary between Glossop parish and the ceased to be crown land about 1678.

Whatever their original function these old crosses and stones must have been a welcome sight to travellers, who had lost the track in deep snow, or when thick mists shrouded the lonely hills. No wonder strangers thought the Peak a dreadful country full of unknown perils. Let us see what Camden had to say in Elizabethan times:—

"There is no more danger now from wolves which in times past were hurtfull and noisesome to this country." He describes the west part of the county beyond Derwent

Pack donkeys at sunrise over Higgar Tor

as one "which riseth high and peaketh up with hills and mountains." Another writer of 1724 speaks of "Three Peakish miles," and those elongated miles have wearied many travellers and ramblers since, over wild tracks in the teeth of the prevailing west wind! Defoe called it "a houling wilderness"!

Peakland remained in splendid isolation until the eighteenth century, a district of Bridle Ways where wheeled traffic could not go. Packhorses were the sole means of transport. Lead was carried by pack animals to some navigable place on the Derwent, or else into Yorkshire, where at Bawtry quite an important wharf dealt with shipments on the River Don. Sheffield cutlery was transported in like manner, and goods coming the other way from Manchester. The Peakland villages had to be largely self-supporting, and only rare luxuries could be brought in from distant parts. In heavy snowstorms they were cut off from the rest of the world, and even in normal times the steep narrow stoney tracks were difficult to the burdened mules, horses and donkeys who trod their patient way. Here are a few of the old routes many of which can still be used in part. From Penistone and the Yorkshire woollen towns a very old path crossed the wild moorland via Cutgate (mentioned in 1571 as Cart Gate), passed through Derwent, over the packhorse bridge, went over a shoulder of the hill by Rowlee Farm, and skirted the north side of the Ashop Valley to Glossop, making use of the older Doctor's Gate in part.

Other ways into Lancashire came via Stannage from Sheffield through Bamford, ascended the lower slopes of Win Hill, winding on to Edale and climbing steeply up to the old Cross already mentioned. A wild lonely stretch of moorland with Kinder Downfall bearing right, eventually descended towards Hayfield. An alternative way to Manchester lay through Chapel-en-le-Frith up the old Stake Road to Rushup Edge, which may still be followed from a point just beyond Barber Booth, Edale.

Sheffield had a route to Glossop from Stannington via Derwent. Besides these main packhorse tracks, the villages were connected by numerous Bridle ways, so that we find Dore and Hathersage, Dronfield and Tideswell, Hope and Ashopton all possessing their special link to name only a few. In fact one cannot walk far in the Peak District without coming across some ancient sunken way.

The fording of the Derwent must have been a dangerous problem at times. The earliest local reference to a bridge,[1] even built of wood that I can find is Yorkshire Bridge in 1693. The frequency of the name " ford " in villages and hamlets marks where the river was crossed in olden times,

---

[1] **Camden shows crossings of the Derwent in his map 1586, but does not state whether Bridges or Fords.**

such as Grindleford, Stoke Ford, Hazelford, Bamford. There are certain places between Bamford and Hathersage where rectangular stones are set closely together in the river bed at shallow spots. Were these once old fords? The earliest kind of bridges to cross small deep streams were made of rude stone slabs thrown across, many of which can be seen on the moors. Farmers still make them to reach fields separated by the numerous tiny rivulets that babble down the steep hillsides. Some were supported by masonry in the middle, a few had several piers to cross a wider stream. The stumps of such a bridge can be seen near the present Cut throat Bridge between Ladybower and Moscar.

Picturesque hump-backed bridges just wide enough to take a laden pack animal existed here and there, like the one crossing a narrow gorge over Bar Brook, and seen from the later turnpike between Baslow and Owler Bar. The historic Packhorse Bridge at Derwent was removed stone by stone before the flooding of the village for the new Reservoir. When sufficient funds accrue, it will be rebuilt at Slippery Stones as a memorial to the late John Derry, Sheffield's pioneer explorer of ancient byways. Another example may be seen at Edale near the Nag's Head, which bridges the Grindbrook.

Shatton Bridge was widened last century from a narrow hump-backed structure, and other Peakland bridges doubtless have a long ancestry if their histories were available. The great bridge building era began with the Turnpike roads, discussed in another chapter. Hazelford Bridge is mentioned in 1820 to replace the old ford, and later was renamed Leadmill Bridge. Mytham Bridge was rebuilt in stone with its double turnpike for the lane to Bamford and the new Sheffield to Castleton road by The Surprise, only to be washed away about 80 years ago in a great storm! After melting snows or a sudden cloudburst on the high hills, the River Derwent becomes a raging torrent, carrying huge tree trunks and debris before it, and piling it up against any obstruction. Defoe speaks of it as " a terrible river, when by hasty rains, or by the melting of the snows the hills are pleased to pour down their waters into its channel . . . " In the days of fords it must have presented a very serious problem and caused the loss of many animals weighed down by their panniers.

The River Noe could also be very dangerous at times. Before the strong bridge was built by Brough Mill, two boys crossed the ford one evening from their farm to go and attend to cattle round an old barn near the Travellers Rest. A violent thunderstorm came on causing a sudden rise in the river. After sheltering for a time they mounted two sturdy farm horses to venture the crossing. By now a swirling flood and gathering night made matters look ugly. The horses had to swim, and the terrified lads were in real danger. At length the struggling animals reached firm footing and safety. This story of old Peakland was related to me by Mr. Jesse Eyre of Brough a descendant of the adventurers. The present bridge was built in 1824, one of the few to carry a date.

Tremendous floods occur still, and only a few months ago the swirling waters of the Noe were about a foot from the top of the arch supporting our Shatton Bridge. Peakland habits do not change much with the years, so far as the elements are concerned!

Slab Bridge, Bar Brook.

VI. TRADITIONS OF CASTLETON

PROBABLY more has been written concerning Castleton than any other place in the Peak. It has become the Mecca of holiday-makers, and so lost some of its original charm. Yet there is much to see of great interest beside the wonders of the Peak; many old nooks and corners that speak of bygone history—tiny windows in houses with ancient glass; little narrow passages leading to mysterious yards, or into the churchyard; babbling trout streams clear as crystal issuing from the bowels of the earth; Inns so old that their birth is lost in the mist of ages. And over all that frowning sentinel on the hill, Peak Castle with its hoary walls.

It is a very romantic village, and no wonder people have written about it for three centuries, and come to explore its wonders long before decent roads were made. Some of the distinguished visitors were disappointed over "The Wonders" and thought them very much exaggerated. The brief account of Camden, first written in Latin 1586 may prove amusing for a start. His book was printed later in English—the famous *Britannica.*

> "Near unto this Burgh (Brough) there standeth upon the top of an hill an old castle, sometimes belonging to the Peverels, called The Castle in the Peake, which King Edward III together with a Manour and an Honour gave to his sonne John, Duke of Lancaster. Under which there is a cave or hole within the ground, called saving your reverence, The Devil's Arse, that gapeth with a wide mouth, and hath in it many turnings, and relying roomes: whatever forsooth Gervase of Tilbury whether for want of knowing truth, or upon a delight he had in fabling hath written, that a Shepherd's son saw a very wide and large country with Rivulets and Brookes running here and there through it, and huge Pooles of dead and standing water. Notwithstanding, by reason of these and such fables, this hole is reckoned one of the wonders of England, neither are there wanting the like tales of another cave, but espcially of that which is called Elden Hole, wherein there is nothing to be wondered at, but that it is of a huge wideness, exceeding steepe and of a marvellous depth. But whosoever have written that there

should bee certaine tunnels and breathing holes, out of which windes do issue, they are much deceived."

And there you have it—all neatly described about 350 years ago! The shepherd lad must have been a daring fellow for those highly superstitious days, and worthy to have joined the present Kynder Climbing Club. He evidently ventured in much further than the great Camden himself, for the " Rivulets and Brookes " are there, together with the vast chambers, which everyone should see.

As for Eldon Hole, it has been properly explored this century, resulting in the finding of a small underground lake. Most people know the story of the first explorer, who was

The Five Arches - Peak Cavern.

lowered by a rope in Queen Bess's time, much against his will, and returned with snow white hair, a jibbering idiot. A thoroughly unpleasant story!

The late Mr. Royse's useful handbook gives all particulars of the various caverns, including the latest find of Tray Cliff with its fine stalactite formations. Let us go back to the village, where history and tradition are so firmly blended. You will hear that " the Druids " once worshipped on the Castle Hill, and their old heathen ritual gave birth to the Garland Day Festivity, which got mixed up later with the oak tree escape of Charles II! Restoration Day, May 29th, still finds Castleton busy with the old celebrations, and the season is not far from the ancient Feast of Beltane, if you wish to pursue this Druid business! Moreover the strange heavy Garland Headdress shaped like a bell, might be traced back by devotees of Druidiom to the wicker cages used for the Druidical sacrifices, in addition to the leafy bower of oak leaves that sheltered Royal Charles!

The church of St. Edmund is supposed locally to date from Celtic Christianity, though no mention of a Saxon church appears in Domesday. The ninth century name of the Patron Saint suggests a strong claim to Saxon origin at least, even if merely a private chapel for the two thanes who are supposed to have resided in a pre-Norman stronghold. The church today is certainly a puzzle, and I disagree with J. B. Firth who called it uninteresting. An unfinished round Norman arch with chevron work leads to the chancel, showing some crude masonry and a suggestion of being transplanted from the castle at one time or another. The font is said to be Norman standing on a Saxon base,[1] and the wooden roof does not seem in keeping. The fine old oak pews are perhaps the most striking feature of the church, the carved knobs varying in style between Charles I, The Commonwealth and Charles II. The doors, many of them bearing owner's names of the seventeenth and eighteenth centuries carved on the original older wood, give that complete privacy so beloved of our forebears. The restored tower is pre-Reformation. The old lead roof was laid 1633.

In the vestry are two old Bibles, a " Vinegar " edition and a " Breechers " Bible, whilst the Vicarage holds an original " Cranmer Great Bible," before the days of chaining these limited copies of Holy Scripture came into vogue. A library of musty old books dates back to the eighteenth century, when Castleton's Library was quite famous.

The Registers go back to 1663, and contain many local names, also the deaths of many miners killed in their dangerous calling. There is a record of a collection made in 1671, " for the redemption of poor English captives from Turkish slavery, by virtue of His Majesty's letter patent dated August 10th . . ." Tyms, Halls, Ashtons, Barbers, Hows, Dakins and Slacks were among the subscribers.

Vicars of Castleton start with W. de Essheton in 1362, and include a member of the Eyre family in 1555. The best-

[1] Not mentioned as such by Cox.

remembered incumbent was the Rev. Edward Bagshaw from 1723-1769. He kept a diary of current events, and was one of the unfortunate gentlemen to lose heavily in the South Sea Bubble. There are many legends surrounding the old church before its restoration about 100 years ago. One concerns a golden altar (or golden altar vessels more likely) given by some king, which Cromwell melted down to pay his soldiers. The late W. D. Shawcross in his valuable booklet, *Castleton and its Old Inhabitants"* (published 1903) gives the Patrons of the Church as " Custodians of the Castle to 1269; Abbey of Dernhill, co. Chester to 1299; Vale Royal Abbey, co. Chester to 1538; Bishop of Chester to 1884; Bishop of Southwell." It will be remembered that the joint parishes of Castleton and Edale were given to the Bishop of Chester at the Reformation. The first chapel of Ease built in Edale dates from 1633, consecrated the following year, and the minister was to receive £10 per annum.

Old view Peverel Castle 100 years ago.

The castle traditionally built by William Peverel, really dates in its present form from Henry II (1176-7), and was knocked about in the Baron's War. In 1403 the grim old keep ceased to be a residence for the nobility controlling Peak Forest, and continued as a prison with a custodian. There is a gruesome story of bones being found walled up near the spiral staircase in some bygone age. After years of neglect, the ruins are now taken over by the Office of Works, and fresh interests are coming to light on the green. A full account will doubtless be published on completion. The good work had a long setback during the war years, when a crane and some gear were blown over into Cave Dale by blast from two parachute mines falling near Odin Mine. The village had a narrow escape that night!

The ghostly old Hall now turned into a Youth Hostel has an ancient wing dating back to the fourteenth or fifteenth century, with some interesting windows. Goosehill Hall with its long avenue and stately gates is another house of interest with a picture that formerly concealed a flight of steps. It was probably built by Richard Torr connected with the Bagshaw family, and the High Sheriff for the county in 1721, Richard Bagshaw lived there. Parts of the house seem older than late 17th century however, and suggest a connection with the former spelling as Gousell, and the Walter de Gousell, who married Matilda de Hathersage long centuries before. Their descendant, Adam de Gousell asserted the right of free warren over Hathersage in Edward III reign.

The Castle Inn is another spot worth visiting, with its creaking stairs and passages leading to upper rooms through low narrow doors of black oak. The cosy taproom has "atmosphere" in the wide fireplace, little deepset wall cupboards, and the shining brass coachhorns slung along the old beams. It was here that I heard from a young mason the story of his finding a Roman coin, and also his discovery of an ancient fireplace walled up in a house, where the same family have lived for four centuries. He told me a more gruesome yarn of a woman buried under a doorstep in 1603. But then strange things do crop up in Castleton from time to time, and nothing would surprise me in a place where Curfew has rung for hundreds of years from the Church Tower.

Yes, Castleton has an atmosphere quite apart from the rest of Peakland—a certain dignity from the time of Royal ownership blended with pride in those local "Wonders," which have put the village on the map as a tourist centre. Castletonians are a proud race, and apt to look askance at newcomers, even from another village, and call them foreigners, but they are a gay hard-working crowd, who love their village fêtes and dances. During the war they raised hundreds of pounds for their local lads and lasses in the Forces, and kept them in comforts.

In olden times the lead mines provided a strenuous and often perilous livelihood. Odin Mine, traditionally worked by the Romans, employed 100 men in 1783, and the mine was mentioned again in 1802 in Mawe's *Mineralogy of Derbyshire*. In 1828 the tithe of lead paid to the church was £60, two-thirds going to the Bishop of Chester. The old-time miners believed in omens, unlucky days and the use of divining rods. On Sundays they wore low-crowned hats, drab coats with cuffs and metal buttons, gaiters and buckles on their shoes. Kinder, who wrote of Derbyshire in 1650 and never finished his book, relates that they ate seven meals a day, had good teeth, and were fond of oats! Wives and mothers at home did the spinning. There was a cotton mill in the eighteenth century near Goosehill.

The old Rope Works in Peak Cavern provided occupation for several families, who long ago dwelt in cottages built inside the yawning cave entrance. Smoke has blackened the roof from these sunless dwellings, which have been described by old writers as the homes of Troglydites (Leigh 1698). The burial of a woman from "Peake Hole" is recorded in the Register 1721. Old engravings of 1727 and 1743 show the cottages, and in a drawing of 1829 two were still standing. The last person to live in the cavern was Mary Knight about 100 years ago. Once a busy hive of industry, the ghostly old posts carry today occasional lengths of yarn and memories of the past. Their spirit of deserted melancholy can best be appreciated on a dismal winter afternoon when one takes a solitary pilgrimage to the cavern portals. The drip of water everywhere, the angry chatter of jackdaws, sepulchral rumblings from the cave's interior, all mingle with an utter loneliness as the ghostly Ropewalk fades in the gloom beyond.

Another eerie impression of old Castleton can be sought by going up the Winnats in moonlight, and hearing the whistle of the wind down the grim pass. The great limestone cliffs seem to tower above you in unfriendly fashion, and the bleak solitude recalls uncomfortable thoughts of Henry and Clara, the runaway lovers who were murdered there by miners in 1768. The unlucky young couple were on their way to Peak Forest, the local Gretna Green. Their bodies were dragged into a cave, and the riderless horses galloped to Sparrowpit.

Yet another old Castleton tale is connected with the small cave at the entrance to Odin Mine. Long ago a man was

Entrance to Peak Cavern

surprised to see light from a fire glowing from within, and on investigation saw a stranger sitting round the cheerful blaze with an enormous bear for company! He promptly fled, and the probable explanation of this yarn came to me the other day when studying a history of Chapel-en-le-Frith.

It seems a certain family in Bagshawe named Shotwell or Shatwell kept several bears which they took round to all the Wakes, even going as far as Rotherham, where the last " Bearward " was worried to death in consequence of a bet made to enter the den at night. He had cut his lip, the bear smelt blood,—and, ended the bet! The old Bear Stake was mentioned in Chapel deeds relating to property at the foot of Terrace Road, and both Bear-baiting and Bull-baiting were grim sights enjoyed by our forefathers in the bad old days.

Castleton keeps its traditions of a great Tournament held by William Peverel, in which an English prince and a Scottish King took part. A family who lived at Goosehill Hall about twenty years ago, possessed second sight, and told me they had actually " seen " this event up on the hill, and also the little Grey Lady of Goosehill! But then, as I said before, one can believe anything strange in Castleton. The casual visitor does not guess the secrets of the old stone houses anymore than the wandering writers of the past, who set down their fleeting impressions of the caverns with a veiled cynicism, called the village " a mean place," and described the inhabitants as touts ready to rush visitors to The Wonders!

No doubt Castletonians were glad of the extra money earned by showing their local " lions." Who can blame them? Moritz who visited the place in 1782 wrote that, " in Castleton there is but little to be earned by the hardest labour." The polishing of the famous Blue John spar and making it into ornaments gradually took the place of lead mining, for the age-old trade is long dead and gone. The Speedwell Mine turned out a false hope, and its long tunnel only carried boatloads of sight-seers to view " The Bottomless Pit," to which the Kinder Club found a bottom, long years after the pioneer miners first cut through into this remarkable subterranean cavern.

Much more could be written of Castleton, but here is one last picture of the ancient place—the memory of a frosty Janaury night during the war, when I left the warm comfort of the local Civil Defence Headquarters. Pale moonbeams bathed the grim old castle on the hill. The village was wrapped in an eerie silence with hoarfrost sparkling on cottage walls. Someone opened a door emitting a glow of ruddy light, then closed it quickly. A dog barked far away, and a fleecy cloud scudded across the face of the moon. This surely was the same Castleton of long ago, and conscious of its spirit, I went on my way, leaving it to dream of The Peverels.

The Winnats Pass in snow

VII. LEAD MINING DAYS IN BRADWELL AND EYAM

"The slave mines," Old-time Miners, Bar-Moots and Lead Smelting, Early Non-conformists, A great-great-uncle's memories of Eyam.

NO Peakland history would be complete without a short account of the ancient industry of Lead Mining. This has been alluded to briefly in connection with Castleton. Let us now walk over the hill to Bradwell Dale and then to Eyam and Stoney Middleton—all limestone villages. Bradwell itself is a grey place with few trees, and steep old roads climbing towards the Moor. In a way it is not unlike Robin Hood's Bay or a Cornish fishing village without the sea, with its closely packed houses clinging to the hillside, and quaint corners everywhere. There are some venerable buildings amongst them, including an interesting old Inn, The White Hart (going back 300 years). Once upon a time the cosy taproom was filled with miners passing their evenings at Shove Halfpenny on an aged ice-smooth table, which still does duty. Miners were merry lads, who loved good ale, sport and music.

In former times a flourishing market was held at the bottom of Town Gate with gay booths pitched on every available space to the edge of the brook, but all that has been changed, and Bradwell folk are getting modernised. None are alive today who remember the donkeys coming down the hill with laden panniers of limestone for the kilns in Smalldale or the one at the mouth of Bradda Dale; nor do they remember the days when local lead was smelted in the Cupolas. The smoke from the smelting and the lime-kilns combined to make a spectacle that filled visitors with awe and wonder. By night the district resembled an inferno with red light from the fires illuminating the dense clouds of smoke. Rhodes described it in his *Peak Scenery*. Today most of the men work at Earle's Cement Works, which once more fills Small Dale with a pother!

Bradwell has its traditions, though few nowadays mention the old legend that their Clan was descended from slaves whom the Romans brought from Gaul and Italy to work the lead. The late O. S. Addy of Sheffield collected several notes from the older generation at the beginning of this century. Robert Bradwell of Bradwell, formerly a Lead Mine Owner aged 88 (in 1907), said he had heard from his father, that miners were descended from convicts from a foreign land a long time ago. He said it was an old tradition, and these people lived in stone huts they built for themselves near the mines, and that was why they differed from other people.

Nobody seems to know the truth of this old story, and probably never will. The same tradition lingered around Wirksworth, where the Romans also mined lead, and where the Hope and Anchor Inn, in the Market Place was built on the reputed site of "The Captain of the Convicts House."—A great deal of water has gone down Bradda Brook in nearly 2,000 years, and the present generation need not worry about their conjectural ancestry! Most of the people in Rome itself were descended from slaves towards the close of the great empire, and some of these slaves were doubtless well-born prisoners of war.

Coming to more recent times, there is a tradition that Bradwell miners enrolled in a company formed to fight for Charles I in the Civil War. Another time, in 1796, they rebelled because they did not want to fight Boney, when wanted for the local Militia. Rioting took place. The miners of Eyam, Tideswell, Castleton and Bradwell and Longstone marched into Bakewell when the Justices were sitting, seized and burnt the hated Militia Papers in a big bonfire, and made a great disturbance, armed with clubs, picks and spades.

About this time many local miners were impressed by Act of Parliament to meet the Bonaparte Scare. Each parish had to find so many men, and lots were drawn in Hope Church. When their own trade was so dangerous, arduous and injurious to health, one might have supposed soldiering would be a welcome change and excitement, but these men loved their freedom, and ignored the hazards of their traditional industry, which was followed from father to son as a matter of course.

Many of the mines were family affairs, owned by the father and worked by the sons. Anyone could lay claim to a lead vein, if he staked his claim and consulted the local Barmaster, churchyards, orchards and private gardens excepted. He had the right of passage to his plot, and could start digging and boring operations protected by a Code of

Laws going back to a time immemorial, and ratified in 1298. All disputes were settled at the big Bar moots held in Wirksworth for the south, and Monyash for the High Peak, usually about Lady Day and Michaelmas; even miners quarrels, which, to quote from Defoe, " may be called the greatest of all the Wonders of the Peak, for they are of a strange, turbulent and quarrelsome temperament and very hard to be reconciled to one another in their subterranean affairs!"

The Barmaster's powers were enormous, taking precedence before civil and coroner's courts. The following account of old Derbyshire Lead Mining has been constructed from William Bray's book, *Sketch of a Tour into Derbyshire and Yorkshire*. The miner claimed his plot by sticking up a little wooden cross called a " Stoter." Twenty-nine yards were then marked out by the local Mining Officer. If the new owner did not start, and another man had a mind to try his luck, he went to the officer and asked him " to nick[1] in." The Barmaster then took 24 jurors to the spot and cut a nick in the cross, and gave the owner notice that he would do this two and three times, after which if no work was started, the claim would be forfeited to the newcomer.

The lead ore when brought to the surface was broken up with heavy hammers on a " knock stone," and then put into a wooden sieve and rinsed in a large tub; the ore fell through and left the lighter rubbish, which was skimmed off and thrown out and taken to the " buddle," where it was again rinsed by a small stream of water, the lead falling to the bottom. What was carried down by the current was washed once more in the same manner. The deposit, almost as fine as flour was called " belland." The beating and rinsing was done by women, who worked nine hours a day for sevenpence!

After all this was gone through, the Barmaster came along on behalf of the Lord of the Manor, who took the proportion due to him varying from one tenth to a twenty-fifth. Before this was done, no lead could be sold. In the High Peak a " Dish of Lead " contained a peck or 16 pints. Nine " Dishes " made a load, and four of these a Horse Load. Pieces of ore the size of a nutmeg were called " bings," and in the fine state it was called " smitham." The ore was run

[1]Later "nicking" of the spindle was done if a mine ceased working that had been started

into " pieces " in Smelting Houses, two of these constituting a " Pig." A " charge of lead " was a hundred-weight, and took from seven to ten hours in smelting. Two men were employed at the rate of about 1/- a day.

The smoke of the lead produced palsies, consumption, quinsies, and a disorder of the internals called " The Belland." Cattle feeding on grass near the Smelting were also effected with the latter ailment, and it was said the

Smelting House. Middleton Dale.

herbage acquired a sweet taste which made the animals eat greedily.

In the middle of the eighteenth century the Quakers introduced Cupolas in place of the unhealthy old Smelting Houses, when injurious fumes were carried through long tunnels in hillsides to a shaft, but in spite of this, many continued to use the former method. The sketch of the Smelting Works in Stoney Middleton has been copied from Chantry's engraving in Rhodes *Peak Scenery,* and shows

Middleton Dale more than 100 years ago. Note also the smoke from a Lime Kiln.

The oldtime miner wore a distinctive dress described by Defoe, who saw one of these strange apparitions climb out of a small shaft from the deep mine. He had on a suit and gloves of leather with a brimless cap, and carried a little basket containing his tools, all of which had names as strange as the terms used in mining. These by the way, are thought to date from the Phoenicians (Glover's *History of the County of Derby*). Defoe gives the weight of ore carried by the man as ¾ cwt., and wondered how he had lifted it up the long shaft, which he climbed on stemples driven into the corners. The author of *Robinson Crusoe* goes on to describe the strange appearance of the miner—" for his person he was as lean as a skeleton, pale as a dead corpse, his hair and beard a deep black, his flesh lank, and as we thought something of the colour of lead itself—" Finally he likens him " to an inhabitant of the dark regions below, who had just ascended into the world of light!"

Sometimes the miners used a limestone cave or natural fissure to reach the lead ore, but they usually sunk long shafts or used old swallets to make lower galleries, getting deeper and deeper in pursuit of the vein. Often the air was very foul, and they were frequently troubled with water from underground streams. Sometimes people undertook to " drive a sough " to carry off the water from their own and a neighbour's mine. If they relieved another's mine they were entitled to a proportion of all the ore got in that mine after cleansing. Pumps were at length introduced like those used in the Cornish Tin Mines, but the old trade was on the down grade, and soon nothing remained but the derelict sad-looking buildings on the skyline, such as Ladywash above Eyam. Today a few miners are employed to get Fluorspar, but Derbyshire Lead Mining is as dead as Queen Anne, and will soon be but an ancient tradition.

A freedom-loving fraternity like the old miners of Bradwell and Eyam were amongst the first to embrace Nonconformity of Worship, and we find them dissenting as early as 1634. Bradwell had no church, and the famous William Bagshawe, *Apostle of the Peak,* spread the Gospel all over the district. Chapels sprang up in about eleven villages, one of the earliest being in Bradwell in 1662. Its massive walls a yard thick would have stood a siege, and in 1715 it was in fact attacked by a Popish mob, whose hopes had been raised by thoughts of a French Invasion to support James III (" The Old Pretender "). They smashed windows, pulpit and seats, and left the inside of the chapel a ruin. The attack took place by night, when the dissenting miners were abed and asleep, otherwise much blood would have been shed. Later the old chapel was damaged by fire and restored in 1754. In 1879 most of the former box pews were removed and new ones substituted.

Methodism also spread rapidly in the Lead Mining Villages, David Taylor conducting " A Mission Tour " in the Peak from Sheffield, and nine years later, John Wesley himself visited Bradwell and preached in the Town Gate close to the old Stocks. The first Wesleyan Chapel was built in " Treacle Street " in 1768. The Baptists also established a small following, immersing their converts in Bradwell Brook by the Holmes. The ceremony was known locally as " The Dippings."

All this time the church people were tramping over to Hope, and not many of them had resisted the calls of rival dissenting worship. However in 1868 Bradwell had a church of its own at last, when St. Barnabas's was built as a Chapel of Ease to Hope. The lax state of the Established Church in the eighteenth and early nineteenth centuries had much to do with the rapid growth of Methodism—the clergy were often the opposite of what their high calling demanded. My brother remembers a story of Eyam[1] told by an aged Great-Great-Uncle who lived there. The parson was too fond of the bottle, and struggling into the pulpit one Sunday morning with difficulty, he looked around and said—" My friends, do as I say, and not as I do!" He was very grasping over his tithes and altogether so unpopular, that one day the vicarage washing mysteriously vanished off the clothes line. The next morning this doggerel rhyme was chalked up on his door:—

" Somebody's stole the Parson's shirt,
What to him could be nearer?
The parish would give five-hundred pounds
If they'd come and steal the wearer!"

---

[1] In dry summer weather the hard church pews were cushioned with sods.

Our Great-Great-Uncle Philemon Andrew of Eyam formed a last link with olden times. He died nearly 60 years ago at a great age, and had lived in four reigns remembering clearly the coronation processions of William IV and Queen Victoria. He had a large number of brothers, the youngest and seventh being christened Septimus. An elder brother, Joseph, fought at Waterloo, and told the family how he had stood beside his horse all through that long day, until the order to charge was given—that last great charge which swept away for ever the dreams and ambitions of Napoleon Bonaparte. This is a personal link taking us quite a long way back into History—an old man that I dimly remember when a very small child, remembered Waterloo, and his father remembered the scare of Prince Charlie's highlanders and the hiding of a grandfather clock and other valuables down a lead mine. It covers a couple of centuries, and so was England's story once handed on from generation to generation, long before history books were made to torment schoolboys!

I am proud of my Peakland ancestry, that we can trace back to Elizabeth, honest yeoman farmers and mine owners. they bind me to the soil and limestone of this corner of Derbyshire to which I have returned like a homing pigeon from a village in the neighbouring county. Is there any other place quite like the Peak?

One more story told by " Uncle Philemon " will illustrate the love of jest and prank in the good old days. On a Christmas evening well over 100 years ago, three young lads were walking up Middleton Dale, and were startled by the sudden apparition of a donkey in the bright winter starlight. They took it along with them to Eyam, and reaching the village two of them tucked Neddy's forelegs into their arms and forced him to walk on his hindlegs up the street. The third boy knocked at the door of a house where a Christmas Party was in full swing. The lads arranged themselves to be in shadow when the door was flung open by a young lady. She let forth an agonised scream as she caught sight of the donkey standing erect. fully believing she had seen his Satanic Majesty on the threshold in the glow of the lamplight! The culprits fled from the hue and cry, (I have my strong suspicions one was the young Philemon himself) and were never discovered.

We suppose the long-suffering donkey wandered back to the Dale, keeping his own counsel.

Those were the days of Christmas Mumming and Guising, when lads went round acting, " The Derby Ram " or " The Old Tup." There were usually six taking part. One dressed in a sack with a real Ram's head represented the Old Tup; the second was a butcher with apron and knife; the third was the boy who carried the basin; the fourth " Little Devil Dout " bearing a broom; the fifth a clown, and the sixth the Collector. There were numerous versions of the ancient Derby Ballad, and I will give the lines as I learned them from my father, which he must have got from the old Eyam uncle :—

" As I was going to Derby upon a Market Day,
I met the finest Tupsie that ever was fed on hay.
Failay, failay, falliddle, ollidle, ay.
The horns upon that Tupsie, they grew so wondrous high,
That when he wobbled his head about they rattled against the sky.
Failay, etc.
The man that killed the tupsie, was up to the knees in blood,
The boy that held the pail, sir, was washed away in the flood.
Failay, etc.

At the third verse " the butcher " pretended to stab " The Old Tup," and the boy with the basin " caught the blood." Then the lad with the broom swept the ground and said— " Here's Little Devil Dout to sweep you all out. Money I want, and money I'll have. If you don't give me money to feed The Old Tup, he will no longer be able to stand up." In Castleton an old woman with a broom represented by a boy took the place of " Little Devil Dout." The slaying of the Tup was supposed to bring benefits on the people, and the play may date according to Mr. Addy, from the time when a ram was cut up for the poor, and even from the days of ancient animal sacrifices. In Derby the horns were sometimes gilded just as the Romans gilded the horns of their sacrificial bulls.

But it was a real Tup from the local Hathersage moors that passed through Eyam a few years ago—the proud mascot of the Peak Batt. of the Home Guards, leading a massed parade that marched through the villages. As part of the medical unit, I had the honour of attending, so I saw the Ram and heard the skirl of Highland pipes—real pipes this time played by kilted pipers to cheer the march, and not the dreaded phantom skirl of Prince Charlie's Highlanders that never came to Eyam just 200 years before!

EYAM CROSS. (from Cox)

And there let us say goodbye to the old Lead Mining corner of Peakland with all its traditions of the past. Much has been written on the history of Eyam and its tragic plague, so I will leave you to read it in other books. Eyam had its poets too, and one of them William Newton, was born at Abney in Cockey Farm, earning the title of " Minstrel of the Peak." The beautiful old Hall, the stocks on the green opposite, and the fine Saxon cross in the church yard preserve Eyam's long history.

Nor must we forget another ancient manor house—Hazelbadge, standing at the top of Bradwell Dale. Once the home of the Vernons who built the surviving gabled wing, it belonged long ago to the Strelleys, a family who fought at Agincourt, and the lands were mentioned in Domesday. Now part of a farm house by the roadside, it forms yet another link in Peakland's romantic story.

Hazelbadge Hall

VIII. LEGENDS OF HATHERSAGE

Little John: The building of the church: Old Industries and Memories

AND so we leave the Limestone Villages for Hathersage nestling under its gritstone edges at the eastern extremity of the old Peak Hundred. Not before time, I hear some say, who may have wondered when this ancient parish would have its turn in our brief sketch of bygone days. But little bits of Hathersage history have already crept into the story—there was Matthew's "indiscretion" over Royal Venison, and his connection with de Gousell; references to Camp Green and old bridle ways, linking Hathersage with the rest of the tale. All these things put together would make a long chapter, if removed from their appropriate sphere.

A few plums still remain however, for Hathersage Pie, and I see one thrust before me—Little John. Long has his grave been a most cherished possession in spite of efforts to disprove the matter. Rhodes in his *Peak Scenery* of 1822, scoffed at the idea, and related the less romantic explanation of a tall man from Offerton occupying the enormous grave in the churchyard. But there are other records to hand concerning Little John. An interesting book about the Stanhopes of Canon Hall, near Barnsley, *Annals of a Yorkshire House* by A. M. W. Stirling, gives a full account of investigations made by Stanhope in 1776, he says—"This famous companion of Robin Hood, who had been a native of Hathersage, was brought up to the local industry of nail making, till his wonderful strength and prowess made him try his fortunes elsewhere. Little is known of his career however till the Battle of Evesham in 1265, when he fought with the rebels under Simon de Montfort, who was defeated. Little John with Robin Hood and many of the earl's followers were outlawed. They forthwith retired to the woods, and escaping the arm of justice, lived a jolly free life till old age overtook them. Robin Hood died at the age of fourscore and was buried by Little John in Kirklees Park, after which Little John sought out his native village, where he wished to lay his own bones. As he approached the Vale of Hathersage, it is said he remarked that his career would soon be ended, and shortly after he breathed

HATHERSAGE FROM THE DALE (*adapted from Rhodes Peak Scenery by Messrs. Northend.*)

Little John's Cottage, Hathersage as it stood 100 years ago.

his last. From that time his great bow with some arrows and some chain armour were hanging in Hathersage church, together it is said, with a green cap suspended by a chain; but when William Spencer became possessed of Hathersage he caused the bow and armour to be removed to Cannon Hall for safe keeping."*(He had married Christiana the sole heir of Ashton of Hathersage and died 1756.) The Walter Stanhope of the story was his grandson . Concerning the long bow, a note says that a Colonel Naylor strung it in 1715 and shot a deer with it. Made of spliced yew, it was above six feet long, tipped with horn, and required a pull of 160 lbs. to draw it.

Captain James Shuttleworth, Stanhope's cousin, caused the traditional grave of Little John to be opened, and six feet below the surface was found a gigantic human thigh bone about 30 inches long. Eventually it was carried off to Cannon Hall. When the old huntsman saw it he shook his head, and remarked—" No good will come to either of ye, so long as ye keep dead man's bones above ground!" They laughed at him, but sure enough both the cousins suffered from a whole series of accidents, until they returned the stolen bone. Sir William Strickland, who was spending a night in Hathersage, and had heard the story from Stanhope, made enquiries from old Jenny Shard, then living in Little John's cottage. She related how when she was about twenty years old, a party of great folk from Yorkshire took away the last relics of Little John.

Dr. Spencer Hall visiting Hathersage about 100 years ago, saw the cottage still standing. The tradition seemed to have been carried on from mouth to mouth. Jenny's father had died at the age of 92, and measured the bone on his tailor's board. Jenny remembered the grave being opened by Captain Shuttleworth, and the story of his bad luck.

The famous antiquarian Ashmole living over 300 years ago, said the bow was suspended in Hathersage Church in 1625, and there seems no doubt that it did, also that it was hanging near the Eyre Monument. If so, might it not have had some connection with former Eyres, who held official rank as Gentlemen Foresters? *The Victoria County History* states in the chapter on Forestry that Edward I made a new rank of Itinerant Foresters known as " Bow

---

* The bow is still at Cannon Hall.

Bearers," who carried a long bow as their sign of office, or else had the bow borne by an attendant. It was a crown appointment, carrying the very high remuneration for those days of a shilling a day, and went to men of knightly rank. This is only a possible explanation, and I have no personal wish to detract from the glories of Little John!

There were no signs of the cap in Cannon Hall in 1876, but it may of course have fallen away into dust by then. Even the cloth caps of a reputed archer will not last for ever to prove old traditions!

It is interesting that the great Dr. Charles Cox went into the Little John story very fully in his *Churches of Derbyshire,* published 1876, and he by no means scoffed. I will quote his summing up of the case—"On the whole the evidence warrants us in assuming that a portion of the weapons and accoutrements peculiar to a forester were hung up in the church, that the said forester (both from the bow and the grave) was of exceptional stature, that both weapons and grave were popularly assigned to Little John more than 200 years ago, and that the said weapons must have belonged to a man of extraordinary fame, or they would not have found such a resting place. This being the case, the opponents of the accuracy of the tradition seem to us to have far more difficulties with which to contend, than those who accept it."

That is the story. Make of it what you will, but the legend will persist as long as Hathersage remains, and why not?—Legend has always played its part in English History. Much concerning our Patron Saint, St. George is legendary, inspiring men to deeds of valiant patriotism down to the present day, carried through a line of distinguished warriors who cried—"England and St. George!" Those who try to slay a healthy legend are taking the romance from our English heritage, so with all due respect to the higher critics let us cling to the Hathersage hero and henchman of Robin Hood. What more fitting resting place for a gallant outlaw than to lie beneath the yew trees in a grave tended by the Ancient Order of Foresters. Sleep on, Little John—Hathersage will keep faith with thee!

And now, standing in the old churchyard at the top of the steep hill, we look with pride at the graceful fourteenth-century House of God, rejoicing that men left such beauty in stone to mark their devotion. The quiet peace of antiquity steals out into the porch to welcome all who would enter for quiet prayer, and meditation on the former men and women who worshipped here. One cannot visualise the past by architecture alone, the human element is needed—the sturdy yeomen of olden days with their wives and bairns, the gentry in velvet, and the humble men who could not read and write, but knew God sent the rain and sun to enrich the land they tilled. The veteran bowmen, remembering Agincourt perhaps, knew the church before their leader, Sir Robert Eyre restored it to its present form. For that is another old tradition—the company of local men who followed Sir Nicholas Eyre and his son Robert to fight with Henry V on the famous field of St. Crispen's Day. The Records Office have failed to give an actual proof, but the story is repeated in most Peakland books coupled with the incorrect statement that Sir Robert "built Hathersage Church."

Here I must refer you once more to our indisputable authority, Dr. Cox, who states that the style of architecture predominating is clearly 100 years earlier, mid-fourteenth century—the Decorated period. The earliest mention of a church occurs towards the close of the reign of Henry I, about the year 1130; Richard Basset in conjunction with his wife Maud, founded the Priory of Launds in Leicestershire and endowed it with the advowsons of no less than seventeen churches, one being Hathersage. No church was mentioned in Domesday, but the Manor of "Hereseige" was held by Lavenot and Levric with two caracutes of land. There is land for two ploughs. To this manor belong four berewicks; Banford, Herct (Upper Hurst), half Offertune and two parts of Middlestone. In it there are two caracutes of land. Land for two ploughs. There are eight villeins and two bordars have ploughs; woodland fit for pannage in places, two leagues in length and two leagues in breadth. In King Edward's time it was worth 60 shillings, now 30 shillings."

The list of Parish Priests goes back to 1281 when one named William held office as Rector. After John Beresford in 1395, they became Vicars, the first being John Rolfe in 1422. Thurstan Eyre held the living in 1442. In all there were 18 Rectors and 25 Vicars. The Parliamentary Commissioners of 1653 gave their report that—"Hathersitch is a vicarage and a parish of large extent," and they suggested that the "hamlets of Bamford, Outsetts, Baucks, Booths and Over Padley should continue part of the parish." The tithes then amounted to £10 per annum.

About 100 years ago, a widescale restoration took place which preserved much of the original early Decorated and later Perpendicular stonework, but which to some extent changed the general character of the building. The architect was William Butterfield who raised the pitch of the roof and the level of the chancel floor, retaining the parapets of the Nave and Aisles, ornamented with crocketted pinnacles. He restored the windows in the Decorated style with the exception of the West window in the Tower which retains its original perpendicular stonework.

The Kempe glass in the East Window of the Church was recovered from Derwent Church before its demolition and the Vestries were added in 1949, a gift from a local family in memory of two sons killed in war.

Some interesting monuments and brasses are to be found in the Chancel, the chief one being an altar tomb to Robert and Joan Eyre, and the fourteen little Eyres of their large family.

There is a strong tradition supported by a former Vicar, the Rev. J. H. Brooksbank that seeds of early Christianity were sown in Hathersage by a missionary monk of the Celtic Church, who built himself a small cell on the site of the present church. Part of a small doorway built into the western wall of the nave may date from this cell to support the tradition.

It has even been suggested that Christian influence began in Roman times, but this is unlikely and quite unsupported. My own suggestion would be that it came during the reign of the Christian Saxon King Edwin in the 7th Century—Edwin's southern boundary is supposed to have been near Bradwell.

A few old cottages still cluster on the hill round Hathersage Church to remind us of the early village. The traditional home of Little John was still standing there 100 years ago, as shown in an old engraving. Now we have only traditions, and the long grave under the yew trees.

Recollections of an older Hathersage are fast disappearing as venerable inhabitants go in turn to their Long Rest. I have been able to collect a few facts however. One old lady remembered going to work at the "Umbrella factory" at the bottom end of the village, connected with Samuel Fox in his early days; and said wire drawing was done through tunnels under the road from the other factory in the Dale to the houses opposite. This factory is of ancient vintage, and made buttons before wire. Rhodes in his *Peak Scenery* describes the descent by the old turnpike into Hathersage Dale by " the old Button factory, once prosecuted in this place with tolerable success, but it has lately declined, and probably may soon be discontinued." The button industry in Hathersage was mentioned in 1795 by Dr. John Aitkin in his *Places of Interest Round Manchester*.

Formerly there was a Paper Mill at Brookfield, and a Needle Factory up the wilds of Outseats near North Lees. The name Leadmill Bridge comes from an ancient smelting site before the present mill, which is mentioned in a Derby Arch. Soc Paper on the Bagshaws and Abney.

Altogether Hathersage seems to have been a busy hive of industry, in addition to the farming that has gone on ever since the early days of " Levenot and Levric." The big straggling parish has had its problems, one of them being the long tedious journeys to the Churchyard when Derwent and Bamford had no consecrated ground for burial, and slow processions followed the mournful farm waggon by steep narrow lanes to reach the Mother Church of Hathersage. An ancient Hearse House stood under a tree near the present Fire Station where funeral parties used to rest the horses in olden times before their last struggle up the church lane. Whilst the beasts were unhitched to munch hay, the mourners retired to an upper room for a meal. This old link with the past has long since disappeared, and its final days coincided with old Bromhead the village constable, who kept order with a stern hand, and watched over "the departed." Like most other village celebrities he combined small farming with his other duties.

In those days the village main street held but two farms, the post office and Hearse House. Squire Shuttleworth had just built a handsome Inn, when Rhodes visited Hathersage, 125 years ago, but the "business of the road was apparently insufficient to support so large and expensive an establishment": so the handsome new "Ordance Arms" remained empty and untenanted for years.

The old village with its Hall dating in part from 1495 clustered round the church and the Dale, and there let us

THE TOAD'S MOUTH ROCK, BURBAGE
(*Photo by Author*)

leave it. The Tudor Manor houses in the outer parish are described in the next chapter, nor shall we forget Jane Eyre's connection with Moorseats, which to some devotees, is the main interest in Hathersage's story!

The present bus route from Sheffield by Fox House Burbage and the Surprise was opened in 1820, superseding the earlier romantic coach roads. If you would explore their stoney isolation climb up Hathersage Dale to the Outseats plateau and on to Ringinglow, or to Yorkshire Bridge passing North Lees.

The march of Time has forgotten them: the wind whispers in grass verges, but the stones perhaps remember the tired feet of horses and the rumble of heavy wheels.

IX. THE EYRE FAMILY. ANCIENT HALLS AND HAMLETS

Padley Martyrs, N. Lees, Moorseats, Highlow, Offerton and Shatton

ONE cannot go far in Peakland today without meeting someone or other called Eyre. The family appears to have been prolific in these parts for centuries, and spread into every village and hamlet; in it history, giving rise to many old local traditions. We have noted two of these legends in connection with Hathersage, and here is a third well known to all Peak dwellers. The story runs that at some time, rather vague as to date, one of the great Eyres living either at Highlow or North Lees, built a Hall for each of his seven sons, to be in sight of one another. Some say it was Robert Eyre, who figures in both the other traditions as the builder of Hathersage Church and leader of a local band at Agincourt. Now Robert certainly had fourteen children, ten or eleven of whom were boys, and we know where some of them went to live eventually. According to Dr. Charles Cox, Ralph Eyre had Offerton, wedding Elizabeth, a lass out of Yorkshire; Robert Eyre had Padley, and was the eldest son; Nicholas the third son, was of Nether Hurst, near Hathersage; Roger the fourth, married his cousin and heiress at Bakewell; Richard, Hugh and Henry died young, without issue; Philip the eighth son was rector of Ashover; Edmund the tenth was of Brookfield,[1] whilst Stephen is mentioned " of Hassop."

Robert Eyre of Padley had seven sons. Three died in infancy, the other four being John, Enstoner (or Christopher), another John, and Thomas. It is all rather a tangle, but Ralph was living at Offerton in 1473, and a Robert Eyre was living at Highlow about the same time, whilst a spate of Halls and large farms arose in Tudor times, associated with the Eyres very soon after, and probably built by them. We find them in both Upper and Nether Shatton, Hazelford, Moorseats and North Lees, and at Crookhill, above Ashopton, all of which are still standing and occupied. Shatton Hall is in fact owned by a present Eyre, after a lapse of years, an interesting link with past history.

---

[1]See Appendix for notes on Brookfield Manor.

The whole great Clan takes origin from the Eyres of Hope in Feudal times, when it will be remembered that William Le Eyr held lands there of King Henry III in capite by service of the custody of the Forest of High Peak. His descendent Nicholas Eyre was father to Robert Eyre of Highlow, the reputed founder of the "Seven Sons" legend. Romantic historians would like to make them a clan of Free-Booters preying on their neighbours' cattle, but I find no real authority for this. They were staunch to the

Pre-Reformation Padley Chapel after restoration
(Sketch by Ray Dyson)

old Catholic Faith however, and often deep in plots for its dying cause. Thus in 1588 came the tragic story of the Padley Martyrs.

Padley had come to the Eyres through marriage in the fifteenth century, and here a younger Robert built a handsome mansion, the most pretentious of all their Peakland Halls. Male heirs died out in three generations, and Anne, daughter of Sir Arthur Eyre married Sir Thomas Fitzherbert of Norbury, who preferred Padley to his own countryside. Like his wife he was a staunch Roman Catholic.

In 1587 the Sixth Earl of Shrewsbury was Lord Lieutenant of the County, and sent a visitation to enquire into the Padley household, which he strongly suspected of being a "House of evil resort." They found Anthony Fitzherbert (either brother or nephew to Sir Thomas), and three ladies, and made diligent search for the heir, Mr. John Fitzherbert, without success. It was suspected that mass was celebrated in the private chapel adjoining the manor, so the following year, the sleuth-hounds of Shrewsbury again visited the spot, or the Earl in person, as some accounts say. Two priests were discovered in hiding—Nicholas Garlick, who had acted as schoolmaster in Tideswell for seven years before being banished, and Robert Ludlam, born near Sheffield. Both had been trained and ordained at the Jesuit College in Rheims. The raid took place without warning on the night of Candlemass 1588, and besides the priests, the unfortunate John Fitzherbert was seized, and carried to Derby. The Jesuits were hanged, drawn and quartered, and for harbouring them, John Fitzherbert was put to death, in spite of his elder brother Thomas's efforts to save him.

The estates were confiscated, and the great Hall at Padley occupied for a time by Richard Topcliffe, Shrewsbury's chief tool in the suppression of the old Faith. They must have been tottering times for the rest of the loyal Catholic families! The Hall fell into ruin eventually, but the ancient chapel still exists after years of use as a barn. It can be seen near Grindleford Station in the restored condition undertaken between the two world wars by devoted Roman Catholics, who hold a touching service there every July. Dr. Cox speaks of three separate entrances connected to the Hall, and a possible hiding hole in a chimney.

Perhaps the most romantic of the old Eyre houses is North Lees above Brookfield. It resembles in part a Border Tower, and is unique in style for this part of the country. William, the second son of Nicholas Eyre of Hope, was the first of the family to live there. (Cox). And this would be at the same period as his famous brother Robert lived at Highlow—mid-fifteenth century. Probably he built it. Opinion differs as to the oldest portion of the house, and records are hard to come by, but notes from the Sheffield Hunter Arch. Soc. suggest the tower was completed in 1594 by Wm. Jessop of Broom Hall, Sheffield, a family connection of the Eyres.[1] This date appears in some plaster moulding in one of the lower rooms, together with some now-indecipherable Latin. The tower is utilised at present by the busy farmers in residence for storage of grain and surplus goods of all kinds. The upper rooms are reached by a spiral staircase cut out of solid elm. At one time a fire occurred in the chief chamber on the second floor, which blackened the walls and destroyed part of the flooring. The upper storey shows a large room with a passage leading behind a built-in screen, down steps to a smaller chamber, spread over with straw; when I explored the tower it immediately suggested the resting place of some weary Jesuit or cavalier fugitives! The whole ancient structure has a strong flavour of romance, which comes to perfection when one mounts to the leaded roof. Leaning over the battlemented parapet a wide vista of hills and woodlands and old grey houses once more fans the flame of " The Seven Sons "—surely this was the place of the old tradition, a fortress set on a hill, a beacon for the Clan!

A long low wing adjoins the tower, which some say is the oldest part of the house—I wonder? The slit windows lighting the spiral stairs are in need of pointing, together with the walls at this junction of the two parts of the building. Let us hope that this grand old stronghold of the Eyres may be saved for many years to come, though their crest has crumbled into dust. A Mr. George Eyre resided there the middle of last century, though the hall was in the Vessey family during the eighteenth century. Nearby are the ruins of a small catholic chapel, built by a Robert Eyre in 1685, when the penal laws against Romanists were held in abeyance by the Declaration of Indulgence. Three years later it was destroyed by a violent Protestant mob, only part of the walls remaining. An underground passage went from the hall to this chapel, and is described as dating from the days of persecuted Roman Catholic priests, who found secret sympathisers in the Eyre Clan. Was there some still earlier building at the end of this passage, or was the exit merely an escape into secluded country?

Here we must leave romantic North Lees and explore its near neighbour, Moorseats. A late Vicar of Hathersage, Mr. Brooksbanks, dated part of this house as thirteenth

---

[1] Hunter's *History of Hallamshire* mentions a Jessop possessed of North Lees in 1561, and later Humphry Savage lived there.

century. Another portion was seventeenth century, blending with the modern additions of 1857. Three small windows on the south wall have been made up, and cause much speculation, as they do not coincide with present storeys, nor is there any access to them. There was a similar window in my brother's old rectory in Northamptonshire, belonging to a room unconnected with the rest of the house. Moorseats has an outbuilding rather suggestive of an old chapel, so had the former Eyres a secret private oratory? Or were the ecclesiastical window styles merely an accident?

The isolation of the place is striking with no proper carriage way, only a steep old grass lane across the shoulder of the hill, passing the more recent farm of Kinder Court, and its interesting tiny cottage of two rooms used by past farm-hands. Together with Carr Head, these lonely homesteads form a tiny hamlet, but Moorseats is the centre piece with its ghost that walks the garden beneath ancient Yew trees, and its more modern connection with Charlotte Bronte. For this is the house where "Jane Eyre" sought the kindly "Rivers" family. You can see the doorway where she stumbled out of the snowy night, and can trace her walk to the crossroads where the coach stopped. My good friends the Misses Hodgkinson, are overwhelmed each year by Bronte Disciples on pilgrimage. Moorseats has been immortalised!

Highlow Hall standing back from the picturesque lane from Leadmill to Abney, is famous for its handsome balled gateway and old dovecot standing in a paddock. The ancient home of Robert Eyre is three storeyed in part and contains a fine staircase. The farm buildings on each side of the yard suggest the former activities of these Peakland squires, a life which is carried on today.

Old Dovecot, Highlow.
(*Author's photo*)

Offerton Hall is reached by a winding lane which descends the wild Dunge Clough, climbs up to Callow,* an ancient farm now used as a Riding School, and then crosses the open moor. The gables of the old Tudor manor house soon come in sight. It is approached through an arch and farmyard. Both externally and internally it is interesting as a sample of period work, though busy farmers have little time these days for showing spectators round the privacy of their homes. Some of the story of Offerton may be gleaned from a brief history of the hamlet. Mentioned in Domesday, " Uftune " contained 2½ caracutes of land under Levric, and land for as many ploughs—also woodland for pannage 9 furlongs in length and 4 in breadth: 5 villeins and 1 bordar had 2 ploughs. In King Edward's time it was worth 20/-. Now 10 shillings and 8 pence, (when a Norman named Warner took possession).

In 1473 Ralph Eyre had Offerton leased to him with the Grange of Abney by the Abbot and Convent of St. Mary's, Rufford. The old boundaries of the Abney estate are very interesting because of the quaint names—" It begins at ye Stoke forth and so goes up Routing Wall sich and so to ye Slacke att the Highlow Head, and so straight over ye moore to a round hill or Knowle calling Berching Hill; from thence to Standing Stone, and so through ye way to ye Dunge Clough Head and following signing Sich to ye Wolfe Pit down along Saundeson Sich, and so to the Burton-Bole; and from Burton Bole following ye gate to Clough Head above Ufferton straight following the Sich to Robin Crosse; from Robin Crosse to the height of Blacklowe as the water falleth from ye Blacklow so to Clusterberry Low and the Straight to ye Archer Stone lying ye south side of Riverage from Abney; and then follow down ye Slacke unto Arminett Well and so to Sylvan Well, and so follow ye water to Starkhouse, following ye water down ye bottom of Bretton Clough, and so to Musford Green, and so to Clustor, and so following ye water to Stoke Forth, and so we ends where wee began . . . " These old Boundaries were " beaten and signed " by 33 persons in the presence of the Abney Steward in 1736. The quotation is taken from a paper on Abney Manor by A. Hughes in the Transactions of the Derby Arch. Soc.

---

* **Oaks from Callow went into the building of Nelson's "Victory".**

In 1570 some of Offerton seems to have passed to a Robert Glossop, gentleman and landowner, and mentioned as a trustee for Hope Free School. It will be remembered that part of Offerton formed a " berewick " of Hope Manor in early Domesday times. In 1658 the following people were living in the hamlet—Abraham Robinson, who was rated for Easter tithes on 4 cows, 2 calves, and a flock of sheep; Edward Glossop and John Leigh (gent) 4 cows, 2 calves and 2 Bee Hives, Joseph Wilson, Ralph Glossop and William Taylor.

Offerton Hall
(*Rough Sketch by Author*)

There is still standing and occupied a very old cottage near the Hall, and down the lane a short way, we find the equally ancient Nether House with its large tumbledown barn and tudor windows. The isolated tiny hamlet bears the mark of great antiquity, a little corner left behind from Elizabethan times, and as we pass down the steep sunk lane present things fade away. A babbling moorland brook is crossed at the bottom, then comes another steep climb between high mossy banks where primroses and shy violets peep in spring. We are treading on worn paving slabs, for the place is " wet with much sprinkling " like a deep Devon lane in parts. We wonder if Robert Glossop rode this way to Hope Church on Sundays, and how often the good church wardens made the pilgrimage, for three from Offerton are mentioned in the Hope List at various times. We are also thinking about Ye Woolfe Pit and Robin Crosse,[1] and the old Archer Stone of the quaint Boundary Record—where are they to be found today, and when was the last wolf killed on Offerton Moor?

And so to Shatton passing Garner House Farm on the pleasant way. Again we feel the shadow of the Eyres, but long before them other memories! "Scetune" was a Berewick of Hope Manor in Domesday 1088, and for 1,000 years men must have tilled the land here, as they do today. By 1208 the name was spelt Schatton, and on May 6th of that year, a Grant was made from Robert son of Ellis de Bradwalle and Alice his wife, to Thos. Foljambe of Teddeswall of a yearly rent of 126 (?) secured upon their lands in Schatton."

In a Roll of Edward II dealing with the Forest of the Peake, the name Peter de Shattone occurs as a Forester in Fee, and in 1305 William, son of Wilhelimina Blanchard of Castiltone, made a grant to Peter de Shattone, Forester, of a rent of 2 shillings, with a day's reaping in autumn price 2 pence, from a tenement in Burgh. Witnessed by Clement de la Ford, Ballins de Pecco, William Hally, Robt de Eyr.

On October 5th, 1551, Henry Wyllasses, Dean, and the Chapter of Lichfield leased for 99 years, the tithes of Bradwalle, Brough-Mill, Offerton, Abney and Abney Grange, Upper and Lower Shatton, Overton and Hylowe to Nicholas Bagshawe of Farewell Co. Staffs. So we see the evolution of Shatton with a glimpse of some of its owners. The Eyres seem to have taken over soon after this, for Robert Eyre is mentioned in a Roll of Principal Inhabitants of Hope Parish both in 1551 and 1571. In a list of Parish Tithes for 1605 "Robert Eyre de Shatton is vallued at IIII shillings." They are not mentioned, however in the list of actual Landowners made 1570. In the Easter Rolls for 1658 Thomas Eyre, gent, was valued at V shillings. The dues from "The Hamblet of Shattons" amounted to eight shillings and eightpence.

As far as I can ascertain therefore, the Eyres were living in Shatton Hall in the sixteenth century, with an occasional

---

[1] Robin Cross was marked on an Elizabethan map of Peak Forest just at a point where Bradwell, Hazelbadge and Abney townships meet. The base has been built into a wall.

mention of one living in Nether Shatton. Was this Nether house the present "Homestead?" It is quite three centuries old, probably older, and once bore the interesting name of "The Counting House," being used for the sorting and counting of the flocks. Part of a low wall opposite the house remains as a relic of those days. It is also recorded that cheeses were stored in a small upper room, now unconnected with the house, except by a trap door from an outbuilding. A huge barn nearby is still used and in good condition. The deeds of the present Dairy Farm go back to Elizabeth's reign.

Old Barns Nether Shatton

An old farm by the ford has been re-christened Wheat Hay during recent years, but this again is a really old house in a charming setting. The long lane leads onwards to Shatton Hall itself between the typical high banks of this part of the world. Some say lanes were made like this for concealment in very ancient days; others that they were old land boundaries like the Saxon dykes; others again that they followed the course of streams, but no stream rises here and Shatton Brook flows at the foot of the moor. Deep snow drifts choke them in winter, and must have made them impassable in former times, as they are today, after a heavy fall. But with the spring flowers they are charming, and no more romantic approach could be found to that glorious Tudor manor house in Upper Shatton.

Nearly 350 years ago John Thornhill of Thornhill came here a-courting Mistress Jane Eyre (a real "Jane Eyre" this time!) All went well with the wooing, because we know they married. Her father was Thomas Eyre and her brother another Robert, who succeeded to Shatton Hall and died 1616. From him were descended the Eyres of Edale and Brough, through the marriage of his son Thomas with Anne Parker of Little Norton. They seem to have kept up the family reputation of large "broods," because eight sons and a daughter figure in the pedigree: Their sixth son Benjamin, is described as of "Nether Shatton"; William the seventh married Miss Lomas of Shatton Hall. I am not clear how the Lomases came into the picture, but the children and children's children of this marriage continued to populate the Hope Valley. A later William Eyre, born 1715, of Brough, began a Carpenter's business in that hamlet, and the family still own it, proud of their long association. They have been Wheelwrights now for 200 years. We shall meet them again in another chapter.

By now we have reached the end of the sunk lane and crossed a field of sheep and lambs towards the old Hall. Nestling snugly beneath the heatherclad hills, the grey gables make a pleasing picture with smoke curling upwards from a peat fire. Ancient farm buildings cluster closely round, and the kitchen entrance faces the yard, where a present-day Eyre is turning out his cows from the Byre. What a glorious old kitchen! One has stepped over the threshold into four centuries back, half expecting a primitive blunderbus to fire through the spy-hole in the stone wall that guards the wide inglenook! This was built for defence, when householders had every reason to suspect late-callers, and strangers were "covered" as a precaution till their business was made known. Yet another protection still exists in the enormous old door key that weighs 7 ozs. This key forms the letter S for Shatton, if looked at end-on. A small sketch is given on another page, together with a diagram of the Spy-hole.

But the most interesting part of Shatton Hall lies through a passage to the old living-rooms and stone staircase. Here there are genuine Tudor windows, consisting of rows of small leaded lights with their original catches for opening here and there. These two large rooms have "atmosphere,"

By courtesy of Alasdair Alpin MacGregor

1. "Highlow Hall"
2. "The Homestead, Shatton"

Photos by the Author

1. Hope Cross on the Moor.
2. February snow in Shatton.
3. Low water in Derwent Dam.

and should surely have a ghost—or is it the spinet of Mistress Jane Eyre that we seem to hear, as she seeks to charm her suitor from Thornhill after his dusty ride?

We go out through the front door into a snug little walled garden with its old yew tree. The Eyres liked to have yews about, and I find I *must* believe that long ago they fought at Agincourt, and made bows from their own "true wood," even though that vital bit of Agincourt Roll is lost to history! Another thing strikes me, as I stand in the little garden—if these old halls can feel in their stony anatomy, Shatton must be mighty glad to know Eyres are living there today, owners of the old stock, who love the grey walls and cherish past memories.

I have before me a list of other inhabitants in Shatton and Brough in 1658, nearly 300 years ago. It may be of interest to some; here it is—Anthony Robinson, Anthony Wood, Ambrose Gardner, Howard Brooke (gent), Henry Crooke, John Ides, Nicholas Hawley, Ottiwell Yellot, Ralph Mellor, Ric. Middleton, Robt. Middleton, Roger Botham, Wife Hoyle, Wife Edmund Barton, Robt. Robinson, Wife Ottiwell Barton, Wife Hardy, Wm. How and Mother, Wm. Marshall, his son and wife. Their farm tithes to Hope Church are shown, and it amused me to know that bee-hives even in those distant days formed part of our local population! I shall think of them when neighbours bees buzz round me in my raspberry canes!

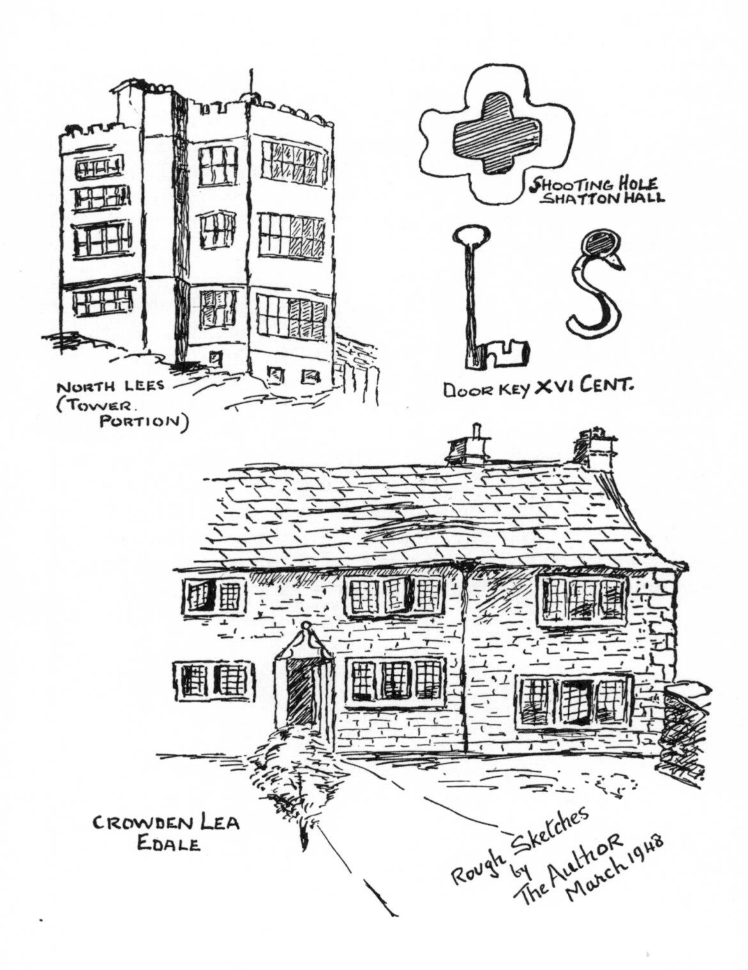
SHOOTING HOLE
SHATTON HALL
NORTH LEES
(TOWER
PORTION)
DOOR KEY XVI CENT.
CROWDEN LEA
EDALE
Rough Sketches
by
The Author
March 1948

X. EDALE LIFE IN THE EIGHTEENTH CENTURY

The Booths. Crowdenlea. Old Account Books. Snowstorms. The Forty-five

IN the first chapter we looked down into remote Noedale from the lofty heights of Kinder Plateau. The time has come to take a much nearer glance round Grindsbrook and the outlying Booths, which make up scattered Edale. It is a lonely corner of Peakland, a sort of cul-de-sac, which had no outlets save steep rough bridle tracks till Mam Nick Pass and the Railway came into being. Winter snows cut it off from Hope and Castleton periodically all through history. Even the Railway gets snowed up in modern times, and last year a local doctor could only reach an urgent case by riding a snowplough engine.

Snow, thunder, rain and wind all seem to come from Edale down the valley. The mountainsides are scored by deep clefts caused by the sudden torrents from cloudbursts, and Noedale weather can change in a few minutes from fair to foul, when the hills are angry. A long battle with the elements and the hardships of hill-farming have bred a sturdy race of folk, who keep much to themselves, and lead a busy life like their forebears did in olden times.

As early as 1329 the tithes from Edale sheep graziers went to Castleton church to swell the coffers of Vale Royal Abbey. There was no ancient Pre-Reformation chapel in Edale, and the good people walked over the hills to the mother church summer and winter alike. Edale's first House of God came in 1663, founded by well-known inhabitants, who furnished a parcel of ground, which had been set aside by the Bishop for a burial site. About 150 years after its erection, it came up for repairs, being in bad condition. In a Brief of 1795 it was described as being " greatly decayed in every part, and much too small to contain the number of persons who profess the doctrines of the Church of England, and who should attend Divine Worship there." In the end the old chapel was taken down and a new one built. The present and third church, dating from 1885, two years after Edale became a parish, is opposite the old site of the former burial ground, and stands in a lovely setting with its background of hills.

The old village clusters round the 1620 Nag's Head Inn, once an ancient Packhorse route. A narrow lane follows the stream up to Grindslow Hall, the home of the Champion family. The scenery grows progressively wilder as we approach a romantic clough and an amphitheatre of jagged crests. The stream is now a Highland burn with cascades and deep pools as it winds down through the heather.

Edale has no startling history, though one feels a great deal lies hidden in the folds of the hills. Once a desolate

SKETCH MAP of the BOOTHS

and wild corner of the great Peak Forest, isolated booths were built here and there for herding cattle and sheep, where grazing was allowed. And it is just like that today—small hamlets of a few houses clustering round farm buildings—still called Booths, and still on the original sites. Lower Booth, Grindsbrook Booth, Barber Booth, Lady Booth, Upper Booth. They have had to be self-supporting in the past—a handful of neighbours to help each other out if sickness or sudden calamity came into their midst, together with the frequently recurring snowstorms.

Seated one March morning on a sunny window-seat in the dining-room of Crowdenlea in Upper Booth, I went back in spirit with the faded yellow parchments and account books that lay scattered around me. They were mostly written in the small neat hand of the eighteenth century, and connected with the doings of past Shirts. My friend, Greta Shirt, the present owner of Crowdenlea, sat near me with her Collie dog, helping me to gather up the threads of past and present. Tucked away in its remote corner few would suspect to find a real Tudor house scarcely changed for centuries, but the Deeds go back to 1587, and little Tudor windows can be seen at the back of the house lighting the romantic small room that contains the staircase and some old furniture. It is a long, low homestead of three rooms in

Tudor Window, Crowdenlea

line, with outbuildings. A stone roof, sagging a bit here and there, falls almost to the upper windows, and a high-walled garden goes down to the narrow winding lane. The walls of the house are immensely thick, making it snug and warm within. As I glanced round the cosy room with its low doorways, massive black Tudor Court cupboard, Jacobean gate-legged table, and the old oak Bible-box dated 1671, I felt little change had taken place. Even the eighteenth-century grandfather clock seemed "modern" in such a setting.

Outside there was no sound but the splash of falling water from the busy Crowden Brook. Great solemn hills bounded the vista—very remote and peaceful; it was "Crowden-lee-Booth," as it had been for nearly four centuries. In my hand was a faded paper of King's Rent for the High Peak in the

Right of his Duchies of Lancaster, dated 1625, the first year of His Majesty, Charles I. It included "Crodenlie Booth, Grymesbrooke, Ollerbrooke and Lady Booth." Another deed dated July 2nd, 1657, concerned the Maintenance of the Army and Navy of the Commonwealth, when Edale had to pay its bit towards keeping Cromwell's Ironsides. We suspect several good Cavaliers chafed at this, for Peakland had strong Royalist sympathies!

There was a list of Founders of the original Chapel of Ease dated 1634, when the building was consecrated. They were Stephen Bright, Robert Hall, Robt. Carrington the first, Frank How, Henry Hall, George How, Giles Barber, Ralph Cresswell, John Hadfield, Roger Hall, George Lowe, Anne Shore and Alice Carrington (joint). These were the men and women who realised man cannot live by bread alone, the first pioneers of Edale's church.

And then I obtained my glimpse of life during the eighteenth century. The story of brief happenings recounted in the long narrow pages of John Shirt's Account Book, which served the part purpose of a Diary.. Under the date 1754, I saw his journeyings and spendings, with little homely bits of news, farm records, and jottings of money loaned.

	£	s.	d.
" Paid for myself and horse going to Wakefield		5	0
Spent at Forest Wakes		1	6
Spent at Tideswell Fair		1	0
Paid John Tym for a quarter of Beef ...		7	9
Paid for Gunpowder and Velvet		1	9
Spent at Hope, myself and Horse			6
For a beast drink and other od things ...		2	6
Sould 4 pecks of Potatoes		1	8
Sould a Fole to Thos. Goddard	1	13	0
Paid for Land Tax and Window Tax ...		15	3
Recd. for 65 lbs, of Buter at Sheafield ...	1	12	6
Lent our Thomas the sum of	6	6	0
Paid church score of 9d. a beast		5	3
Some time sould 12 ewes	4	0	0
Sould 23 stone of wool	10	7	0
Paid Hedborrow score to Samil Barber ...		3	9
Paid masons for 26 days' work	1	4	0
2 days Nat. Philemon one day ith hay ... (Amount not recorded)			

Lent Micah Roobottom a ginney	1	1	0
Lent Jonathan Hadfield	2	5	0
One load of meal sould to him	1	5	0

Then follows a personal entry written at the top of a page—"Jacky went to school Jan. 7. Mark gave over going to school." I understand they rode up the Stake Pass to Chapel-en-le-Frith, and were probably weekly boarders. Then came a note of selling Lambs' wool to "Abull Hide," and on June 23rd, 1774, an amusing note about a farm-hand: "James went home badly. August 21. James came here againe. 23 Dec. James fell ill again. Reckoned with James Broadhurst and paid him £3." (James had no Sick Benefit in those days!).

There is mention of a maid servant, Mary, who received £3 a year and her uniform of those times—a scarlet cloak, blue dress and pinafore with a pair of boots. She had her own staircase up to bed, which is now walled up near the old-fashioned kitchen.

In 1748 when Parson Bagshawe of Castleton kept his Diary, the Shirt's relations the Foxes appear to have lived in the old house next door for the Diary records: "On May 30th being Edall Wakes, I went to Crowden lee Booth and dined with Mr. Fox of the Yate, and drank tea with Thos. Creswell of the same Booth. Neddy and Isaac Hall went along with me." They seem to have had quite a good time on the whole in the eighteenth century with their visits to Wakes and social gatherings—it is interesting to see they drank Tea, which was then only just becoming fashionable. By the way, "The beast drink" in John Shirt's book referred to a colic drench and not a pint of ale from the local, as might be inferred!

One can picture the cosy Christmases at Crowden-lee Booth, with punch bowls and Frumetty and the waits singing the famous old Edale carols; but the first performance of Handel's *Messiah* given in Hayfield Church, 1786, was billed on September the 25th very wisely, before the snows came. Greta Shirt showed me the original programme, with the price of gallery seats 1/6, and the Bottom of the Church 1/-. There were "Hautboys, violins, flutes, buffoons, trumpets and drums" to augment the singers, and it was doubtless a great occasion in Peakland.

Farming duties were not the only thing in the day's work. Before Parish Councils managed local affairs, village "Overseers" were chosen from the respectable inhabitants, who looked after roads and collected various payments and taxes. Thus John Shirt and a neighbour, Ralph Creswell, about 100 years ago made a new road to Upper Booth and The Lee (near Jacob's Ladder), and constructed two cart bridges. This office of Overseer was very ancient, and is mentioned in a History of Chapel-en-le-Frith. An explanation of the word "Headborrow" or "Headborough," as sometimes spelt, says: "The Headborough was head of a frankpledge in borough, and had a principal government within his own pledge." He was also a kind of constable. "House Row" was another term in common use in northern counties, for a system by which the inhabitants were elected to serve in regular rotation the various compulsory parochial offices, such as churchwardens, constable, etc. Suffice it to say that the chosen man was boss of his village with certain onerous duties to carry out.

In 1768 there was an Assessment "for the Headborrow of Edale to colect twelve penny lay throughout the said hamlet towards paying the Militia Money charged, etc." Thirty-four local names follow including six Eyres and seven Champions.

The same sort of life was going on in other remote hamlets of Peakland. In Abney, for instance, John Bagshawe of Abney Grange kept a Diary for about ten years, and his jottings for 1700 include:

"May the 12 account of Mean Charges.

	s.	d.	qrs
Paid for ter (tar) and ole		8	0
For talors (candles)		3	0
for a Pigg	18	6	0
for spenses at Chappell Fair		1	0
for smith work		3	0
for a calfe	5	4	0
for coles	1	2	0
Easter dues	1	11	0
for Land Tax	2	0	0

Two other interesting items are "Headborrow score 1/8, and Poor score 8d."

He fetched his "cole" from an open pit on Stanage Edge, which is mentioned in other old records. Clothing was supplied by weavers and tailors who came round the country-side to work in houses,[1] the people buying their own hemp, flax and yarn, also flannel and cloth, often brought to the door by pedlars with pack-donkeys.

Another interesting old Account Book I have examined belonged to Martin Eyre in 1793, a member of the family of Wheelwrights at the hamlet of Brough. He seems to have gone into big business, and migrated to London for a time. Here are some of the items :

> I have shipped on board the *Nonsuch*, Capt. Cobb, by the order and for the accompt of Hans Van Dealen of Amsterdam the following goods marked and mentioned as per margin :

	£	s.	d.
3 pieces of Broad Cloth at 5/- per yard ...	45	0	0
20 pieces of stuff at 2/- per piece			
30 pieces of Long Silk at 4/-	135	0	0
40 Hogsheads of Sugar	12	10	0
My commission on the whole	15	7	2

Martin Eyre appears to have acted as Banker and handled large sums on interest, but things did not always go well with him, for another entry records : "I have this day received advice that ship *The Dragon* is castaway being on her voyage to Hamburgh. She is Total Damage £165 14s. of which lofs is to answer for James £100 and I the Rest which is £65 16s." (Another 2/- seems to have crept in somehow !) The prices of goods are interesting to compare with those of the present day, and here one might note that Bohea tea was selling at 8/- a pound, though tobacco was only 1d. an once !

Journeys and social calls were alike undertaken on horseback, and the first heavy, lumbering coaches to Manchester only came with the 1757 Turnpike up the Winnats. Yet our forefathers certainly got about, judging from their various diaries, and they rarely failed to visit Wakes and Markets. In winter they prepared for snowstorms by laying in ample stores that would have stood a siege. There was no dropping food by aircraft to outlying farms—they had flour

---

[1]They must have had a job running the tape measure round John Shirt's five foot waist ! He weighed 24 stone !

and meal, home-fed beef and pork in plenty, made their own cheeses, often from ewes' milk, and had enough fodder put by for the beasts, who lay snugly stalled in dry bracken. The harvesting of bracken was a great thing at Edale, and is still done today. Sledges are used on the steep hillsides where wheeled carts could never get.

Speaking of snowstorms, I have collected records of a terrible one as far back as 1635 when many of the deer in Peak Forest perished. 1674 and 1692 were also mentioned. in the first one a grazier named Barber and his servant were

Looking back on Barber Booth in snow

buried in the snow for months on Win Hill. In 1711 a woman was frozen to death near Edale End, and March, 1716, "saw a most severe snowing and driving that hath been seen in the memory of man in the High Peak." In 1749 Parson Bagshawe of Castleton was hindered from going to Sheffield on horseback by a great snow that fell in the night. But Peakland folk "took it," as they do today, and no Skiers flocked to Edale for winter sports. The snows of 1947 was perhaps the heaviest of all time!

Now and then startling outside news set tongues wagging, for instance when Bonnie Charlie led his Highlanders to

Derby in 1745 with vain hopes of a crown. Rumour had it that the gaunt, hungry Scots in their ragged kilts ate little children and stole everything by the way. Cattle were driven to secret folds of the hills such as Bretton Clough, whilst in Eyam I know of a grandfather clock that was hidden in a lead mine! The line of march was miles from this district, but a few stragglers did find their way, perhaps deserters or those on foraging parties. A Highland claymore and dirk[1] were dug up near Hathersage, and I have often fingered them on the walls of Hathersage Hall. Another story of the "Forty-Five" comes from Hope Woodlands. A lady told the late Dr. Porter of Hope that her father had remembered hearing his great-uncle, a farmer, speak of a visit from the followers of Prince Charles Edward to the Woodlands, and how the farmers buried their silver and other treasures on hearing of their approach. My own father had a similar story from his great-uncle in Eyam, and these old memories bring the eighteenth century so much nearer, together with the well-kept Diaries of everyday life.

The Rev. James Clegg, minister of Chinley Chapel and a doctor, kept a record of those hectic days when the Highlanders were advancing. I will quote some of it, because Edale, just over the hill, must have been feeling a like panic:

> "December 1st, 1745.—The Rebels left Manchester in ye morning and entered Macclesfield soon after noon, and lodged there all night.
>
> "December 2nd.—The Rebels rested all day in Macclesfield, but soon had eaten up their provisions, and made filthy and ruinous work in their houses.
>
> "December 3rd.—The Rebels left Macclesfield and took the road to Congleton, Leek and Ashbourne."

December 4th was a very long entry about sending a man to Derby, who saw the Rebels marching and was in danger of being pressed for service.

> "December 7th.—A rumour prevailed that the Rebels were just coming upon us, which occasioned great confusion."

However, the expedition was already in retreat from Derby towards Scotland, and the next is:

---

[1]See note in Appendix.

"December 10th.—Ye Rebels have all returned to Manchester on Tuesday. They took several persons with them from Stockport. Blessed be God ye Silk mill is safe."

Almost two hundred years later, Peakland had something worse to worry about, when the Battle of Britain was being fought, and the newly formed Home Guards of the Peak Battalion were drilling on those tense long summer evenings, just as their forebears had done for the Spanish Armada scare, and the expected Buonaparte invasion. Edale had its toll of crashed bombers too in the Great War, and some of us will long remember arduous climbs in the middle of the night, when a homing plane failed to make base, and "had it" amongst the cruel peaks of Kinder.

My long day at Crowdenlea is nearly ended, and after eggs for tea from Greta's fowls I walk back the long two miles stationwards. The wind is snell and dusk falling. After Barber Booth a patter of rain comes down, and I am glad to reach the quiet railway waiting-room. There is nobody else on the platform but a young porter, who tells me the train will be late leaving Chinley. The dim oil lamps bob up and down in the freshening wind, which howls in the cracks of my shelter. How lonely it is, and how typically Edale, recalling many dark stormy evenings during the war. At long last the young porter's lantern appears again with the welcome news the train has left Chinley. (His name by the way was Eyre!) We chat for a few minutes about Civil Defence days—and his later service. We agree that Edale has not changed much since packhorse days, and hope it never will. Then the train comes cantering down from Cowburn Tunnel, and I wonder what "Little Jackie" would have thought of it two hundred years ago! Would he have preferred his long ride to school over the Stake Pass?

XI. DERWENT AND THE WOODLANDS

Abbey Grange and Ancient Chapels. Derwent Hall. Ancient Farmsteads. Old Methodists. Bridle Roads. The Coming of the Waters

THERE was an old rhyme about Peakland villages which ended up " And Derwent for Water." Was this prophetic of the days to come, I wonder, when a vast series of reservoirs would cover the valleys, sweeping away ancient farms, a church, an old hall and several bridges? The former inhabitants would rub their eyes in wonder and consternation if they suddenly returned to see the dams and modern viaducts! Perhaps it is as well they have passed to their Rest, knowing things only as they were. Future generations will know it as today, ignorant of its story, unless some legend starts about bells ringing under water, like they say in Cornwall and the lost coastline of Holderness!

What was Derwent like centuries ago, and who lived there? It was not mentioned in Domesday, and must have been wild waste land in the early days of the great Peak Forest. A king is supposed to lie buried on the moors. Yes, Early Man knew it and left many cairns and barrows ; a Saxon Boundary Ditch is shown on maps as Seward's Lode, mentioned in 1425. It lies north-east of Nether Hey beyond Abbey Clough.

The first reliable records of Derwent concern the acquisition of land and founding of an Abbey Grange by the Canons of Welbeck in the reign of Richard I on the east bank of the present Howden Reservoir. The land is described as " the pasture of Crookshill, the woods of Ashop up to Lockerbrook, and from Lockerbrook up the valley of the Derwent even to Derwent Head." This grant of land was confirmed by King John to the Abbey, and again later by Henry III. It then formed part of the Manor of Hathersage. On the death of Matthew de Hathersage at the end of Henry III's reign, these estates were divided between two co-heiresses. Nigel de Longford, son of Cecilia, co-heiress of Matthew de Hathersage, gave to the Abbey of Welbeck the remaining lands in Derwent, on which The Grange itself was erected. It still survives in Abbey Farm.

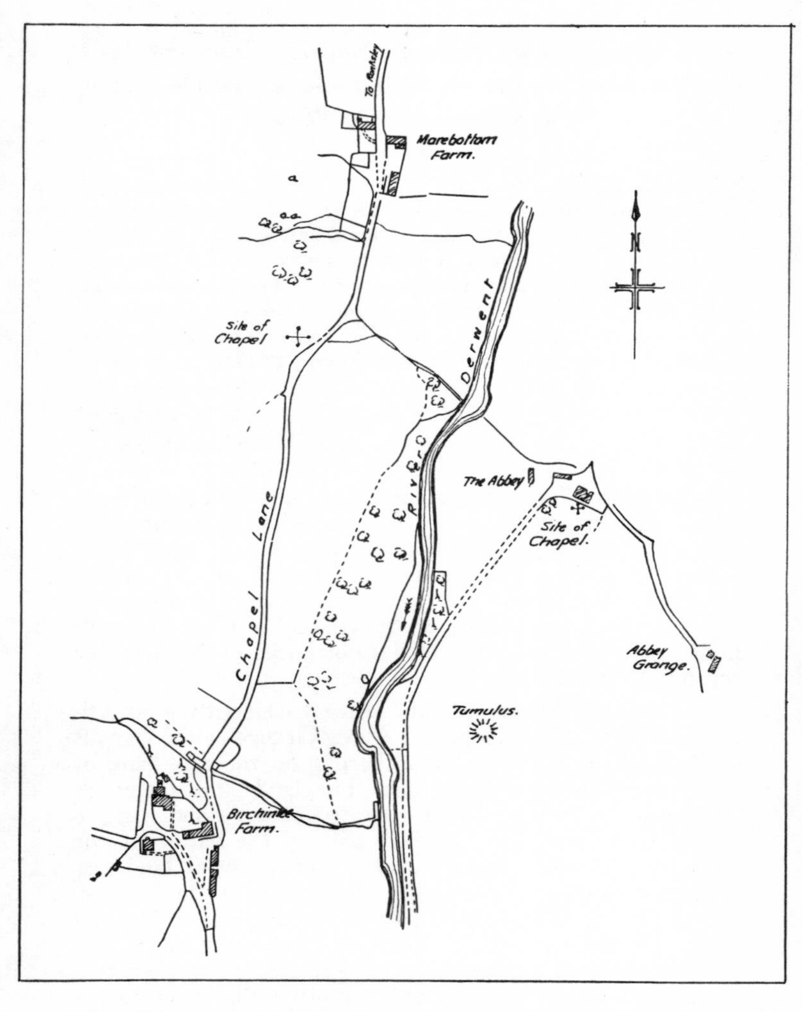

Map of area around the Abbey and Old Chapel sites before the Reservoirs were made, Derwent

A valuation made in 1299 gave the Welbeck Abbey estates at Crookhill as £7 17s. 4d. The Grange had exemption from the Pope in the payment of tithes of the newly tilled lands, which they had planted with vegetables with their own hands; of the increase of animals; of the gardens and of the orchards. We can picture the old monks busy with their spades long ago. They also built four chapels, two of which were Wayside Chapels for the use of wayfarers. One was near Maresbottom and the other up the Woodlands. A third chapel belonged to the Abbey Grange buildings, and the fourth, at James Chapel near the mill and hamlet, continued in succession to the church that has just gone under water. The monks built a bridge over the Derwent opposite the Grange, and another one on the site of the Packhorse Bridge that everyone remembers so well in its charming setting, near the Hall.

The Wayfarer's Chapel in the Woodlands stood by the side of the old Roman road, where an ancient wayside cross stood, the pillar of which was used until recently for parish notices (Cox). The name Friar's Walk retains a memory of this chapel. Possibly a monk resided there to succour benighted travellers. The chapel near Maresbottom was called "The New Chapell," so may have been built rather later, and lasted longer, because it was shown on Saxton's Map of Derbyshire (1557), on Speed's Map (1610), and on Ellis's Map (1777). On an eighteenth-century map I have reproduced at the beginning of this book, "New Chappell" is shown in a position suggesting the old chapel up the Woodlands, but then the Devil's Hole is shown a long way from Castleton, so this may be an error likewise!

Old Ordnance maps give a "Chapel Lane" going from Maresbottom to Birchenlee, which retains the old tradition, and it is said the stumps of the monk's bridge used to be seen in the river before the dams were made. And now the later Ouzleden Bridge has gone too! On rare occasions it can be seen in times of drought when the water is low.

We do not know why the monks chose the secluded Derwent Valley far from their parent Abbey, but the choice is in keeping with all the other beautiful sheltered sites of monastic occupation. They remained in quiet possession until Henry VIII dissolved the Monasteries, Abbeys and Chantries in a royal effort to support his title "Defender of the Faith," thereby enriching his coffers, and rendering many poor pious monks homeless. So the old order was changed and the chapels around Derwent fell into decay. But the mill went on grinding for many centuries, almost within the memory of old inhabitants. After a time the Abbey Grange was turned into a farm, and its chapel, perhaps, into a barn or byre for cattle. Only St. James's Chapel remained for religious worship, now of the established Protestant Church, and so continued until 1757.

In an account of lands sold in the reign of Queen Mary, the property of Derwent is mentioned and " the leads, bells and advowsons " were exempted from sale. The Parliamentary Commissioners of 1650 described Derwent as a parochial chapel in the Parish of Hathersage with an income of £8. They recommended it should be made a Parish Church. In 1688 the Earl of Devonshire paid through his agent, Mr. Greaves of Rowlee, £5 as a gratuity to the Rev. Mr. Nicholls for his services at Derwent Chapel. Dom Philip Hutton is mentioned as the curate of Derwent in the Hope Parish Register, February, 1707. The Rev. Robert Turie, curate of Ecclesall and assistant minister of Sheffield Parish Church, bought back the alienated Abbey Farm, and it was added to the living of Derwent in 1722. The Balguys gave the font in 1670 which bore their arms. For a time it served as a flower-pot in the Hall gardens in later years, before its restoration to the new church.

There is a grim story told of some Scottish soldiers being imprisoned in the chapel and starving to death. Some think they were part of the defeated army from Preston in 1648, when 300 more were locked up in the church at Chapel-en-le-Frith, on their long march to London as prisoners of war. Others think they were a wandering band of Prince Charlie's Highlanders in 1745—perhaps the very men who had come down the Woodlands and frightened the farmers, as recounted in the Edale chapter. It is a gruesome tale!

The second chapel was smaller, and from contemporary accounts an ugly building with round-headed windows and a square bell turret at the west end. It was removed in 1867, and the Derwent church, which many remember with affection and interest, was built. The tower and spire were added in 1873. (Cox's *Derbyshire Churches.*) The foundation stone of the second chapel was built into the east wall of the chancel, and many old fourteenth-century stones from the first chapel were likewise used. An old sundial used to stand in the churchyard, made by David Rose, a Welshman who came to live in the Woodlands, and was both clerk and schoolmaster at Derwent about 150 years ago. He also made the sundials in Hope and Hathersage. It is said his mother lived to be 105.

And now nothing remains of the church. A sheet of water covers the hallowed spot where Derwent people worshipped. Stone by stone it was taken down in preparation for the new dams. Water washed about the foundations: for a time the

Old Packhorse Bridge, Derwent
(*Sketch by Ray Dyson*)

gaunt tower and spire stood up, only to attract crowds of curious sightseers—now all has gone and Derwent church is but a memory. . . .

After the Dissolution of the Monasteries the estates passed to the Cavendish family. It was not until 1672 that Henry Balguy built the magnificent Hall, so well remembered as a Peakland beauty spot. He also rebuilt the old Packhorse

Bridge of the monks, which was described as very decayed. Originally the Balguys lived at Aston Hall, and were also at the old Hall of Hope in the seventeenth century. Some of them had migrated to the Woodlands. Henry Balguy is mentioned as an attorney, and must have done well in his profession. A former Balguy had been a Member of Parliament in Elizabeth's time, and they were always cropping up in Peakland history.

Later the Hall at Derwent came into the hands of the Newdigate family, and in 1886 it was purchased by the Duke of Norfolk. The original building was enlarged and a private chapel added. A Roman Catholic chapel was also built above the village, so the Old Faith still lingered in the district. The Hall's final lease of life saw its grey walls a Youth Hostel, opened by the Prince of Wales in 1932. The handsome balled gateway and flight of circular steps welcomed lads and lasses with rucksacks instead of visitors in old-time lace and velvet. But the Balguy's former home was under doom of destruction and had more to lament over than the noise of heavy young feet along its corridors! I remember taking a friend over the Hall in 1938, in the first mutterings of the World War. Mr. Rouse, the dear old vicar, was with us, and we all felt the sadness lurking in the delapidated rooms, the chapel, and the wilderness of tangled garden. It was a summer evening with brilliant light and shade: the birds were singing their vespers, and melancholy bumblebees droned through the sweet air, "making honey while the sun shone," for one day their garden would be no more. Ancient trees of huge girth stood there dreaming of the past, and dreading the whispered threat of the woodman's axe. Yes, it all felt very tragic!

Many ancient farms were likewise under doom, several of them going back for centuries like the families who dwelt therein. Crookhill goes back to the fifteenth century, once the home of Adam Eyre, and generations of Eyres until about 1825. Barbers of Ronksley and Marebottom figured in Hope Parish Easter Roll for 1658, and before that in 1546 we find Thomas Barber of Ronksley and another Thomas of Westerden; Henry Balguy (gent), Adam Eyre, Edward Barber (Captain), Thomas Eyre of the Ridge, and Thomas de Alport: all giving big tithes to Hope.

Westend Farm situated on a Packhorse route to Glossop via Rowlee was a Rest House for travellers long ago. Some of these old places may in fact go back to medieval times. Thirteen of them were rendered desolate for the first building of the reservoirs, and their names exist on maps only. The Greaves of Rowlee were there for generations. In the seventeenth century they were mentioned as agents for the Cavendishes. The last one left about forty years ago.

Grainfoot was another interesting house, and contained an enormous kitchen, built specially for Hunt breakfasts, when the Penistone hounds hunted that way. When last I saw it the new dam was lapping within a few feet of its deserted walls. Cocksbridge, Grimbocar and others have gone too, and Crookhill now stares down on a cold "sea" and long white bridges. Only the Woodlands remain much the same as before, an immense valley of semi-wild country, with Cloughs going up to the heights. Over 100 years ago the Duke of Devonshire encouraged agriculture in addition to the age-long sheep-farming. The new Turnpike made things easier, and about 1824 a cart track was made from below Alport Bridge over the hills to Hope, following the old mountain Roman road. We suppose this would be used by two Edale farmers, who were fetching drag-loads of timber out of the Woodlands about the year 1830. Just below Hey Ridge there was an awful catastrophe on the homeward journey. A flood of water came rushing down the Ashop valley, which swept away men, horses and timber. Some time afterwards the men's bodies were found ten miles away at Grindleford. One had a leather belt still round his naked body containing 70 sovereigns!

Methodism took early root in the Woodlands, where people were so cut off from their parish church in Hope. They held prayer meetings in farms and later at the Snake Inn; the early devout innkeeper, John Longden, has already been mentioned. Their chapel was not built until 1868. This same John Longden, and famous Woodlands local preacher, set out one Sabbath in 1815 to preach at distant Tideswell, only to find on arrival that his flock had all gone off to see the local murderer Anthony Lingard hanging from the gibbet at Wardlow Mires. He followed and preached a forceful and moving sermon at the gruesome spot. By then the Wesleyans were getting their circuits established, and some of their early persecution ceasing. We hear they were pelted in Eyam and stoned in Tideswell, whilst in

1776 the Rev. T. Seward boasted he had driven them out of Eyam down to Grindleford. Ashopton got its Wesleyan chapel in 1840; Bamford in 1821.

Ashopton was a quaint village with its inn, old tollhouse and bridge and few cottages all lying snug. Once it was known as Cocksbridge, and so named in the coaching lists[1] of stopping-places between Sheffield and Glossop. Over 100 years ago the bridge collapsed, killing several men. Old folk still talk of the disaster. The road from Derwent to Ashopton made by the Newdigates in 1824, and the turnpike on to Bamford somewhere about the same time, superseded the old local bridle lanes. Another road, known as Mortimer's Road, was started in 1771 from Yorkshire Bridge to Penistone, but never got far. Part of it may be seen near Ladybower. The inn at Ladybower dates from 1821, though it had been a sheep farm long before that and is mentioned in mid-sixteenth century.

But it is in the old bridle roads that romance lingers, the tracks that wandered over wastes of moorland skirting high hills and dangerous bogs, slipping down cloughs, fording streams. Charters of the early fourteenth century mention "the common way which leads from Sheffield towards Darwent." The old road from Bradfield passed beneath Crow Chin and the Old Woman Stone; the Sheffield to Glossop via Stannington forked at Mill Clough; that ancient way from Penistone to Ashopton and Derwent via Cutgate (called "cartgate" in 1571), descended to Slippery Stones and divided each side of the valley. Stones were set up over the bleak ridges to guide travellers in snow. The later Duke of Norfolk's Road followed time-honoured tracks to give Derwent and Woodland farmers a better route to Penistone market, and the hounds came that way to Grainfoot. To feel utter loneliness take one of these moorland walks today and think of the past. Small wonder that the good monks ministered to wayfarers!

A few words now on the Coming of the Waters that changed the face of the Derwent valley. The first two reservoirs, Howden (1912) and Derwent were completed by the Derwent Valley Water Board in 1916. Their fort-like

---

[1] These were Lidgate, Rivelin Mill, Surrey Arms, Cocksbridge, Lady Clough.

towers and massive walls make a striking picture rising fron. the water, and the new road along the west bank made by the Water Board has been a favourite run for motorists. It terminates near the site of ancient Ronksley Farm, passing Birchenlee, once known as "Tin Town" when the navvies and their families dwelt there for years during the dam-making. Derwent village remained an undisturbed beauty-spot until the war years, when demolition began gradually, starting with the felling of timber. Then the big white viaducts went up foot by foot inside their towers of scaffolding. An enormous new wall was also under construction across the valley from Win Hill to the Filter House.

The day came when little Ashopton and many farms were vacated and Derwent fared the same; roads were diverted, everywhere there was chaos and ugliness for a time, then by Herculean labour all was straightened up, the vast new Dam filled itself from the water shed,[1] and the flags went up ready for the King and Queen. Their Majesties performed the opening ceremony on September 25th, 1945, amid vast crowds of loyal spectators—it was a great day in Peakland History.

And now after winter rain and snows we have the green valleys filled to overflowing. Old roads and old foundations lie fathoms deep. A chill west wind whips up the water into little blue-grey waves—a wild sunset over Win Hill reflects pink and primrose lights in the new lake, or a single shaft of gold falls through the misty stillness of a frosty afternoon in winter. Yes, it is beautiful in all weathers this man-made Lakeland, and perhaps sometimes we forget the past—the steep wooded lane down into Ashopton with the tree-lined river babbling and swirling over boulders—the grey cottages and the old corner we once turned for Derwent, before the waters crept up the church tower and the ruined Hall. The exiles from these lost villages are comfortably housed in the picturesque stone cottages built by the Water Board at Yorkshire Bridge, some of them will talk now and then about the old times. Old Mr. Tagg told me some interesting traditions about Lead Smelting at Broadhead Clough, Cold side, near Slippery Stones, Howden Clough, and in Millbank

---

[1] **It holds 6,300 million gallons. Total length of three dams about six miles.**

Plantation. He maintains lead was brought from the limestone district to these desolate spots, but he had no idea when it occurred—had it something to do with the Canons from Welbeck? These old abbeys sometimes forged iron in ancient times, so it is not improbable. They would need lead for their chapels.

Mr. Tagg also talked of the old bracken burning for use in silver polishing at Sheffield cutlery works, and he said the former people of Derwent paid rent in Hazel Nuts, which was used for a dye. All these old traditions are worth preserving—we shall not see Derwent and Ashopton again!

Nor shall we see Mr. Tagg again, but the glorious story of his faithful sheepdog Tip will live on, and her wonderful eleven weeks, vigil over the body of her beloved master, when he perished on the lonely Derwent Moors in the bleak winter of 1953-54.

For this deed Tip received the Bronze Canine Medal at the Bamford Sheepdog Trials 1954. Since then, she has passed on to the Happy Hunting Ground. Her portrait is one of my treasured possessions.

* * * * * *

My task is done and Peakland's story told in brief. Much more could have been said, and much more has been written in other larger books. If I have aroused a fresh interest in the antiquity of our corner of Derbyshire, and a love for the old grey churches and houses, and the people of the past, I shall not have written in vain. There is still a great deal to be discovered, and I shall go on with the hunt—perhaps you will help me.

APPENDIX

ANOTHER TALE OF THE '45 has reached me from a lady in Sheffield, possibly throwing light on the Highland dirk and claymore found near Hathersage (see page 83). The leader of a straggling party of Prince Charlie's army broke his leg on the moors behind Hathersage and was carried on a hurdle to Hallam where a famous Bone Setter, George Worrall gave him skilled attention. The invalid was hidden carefully until sufficiently recovered to escape, when he was safely conducted to Doncaster with his servant. The grateful Jacobite well rewarded his kind benefactor, and the story goes that he reached home safely. Meanwhile two other Scots of the little party dressed as Drovers, helped to drive a flock of sheep to Sheffield town, and guided by a shepherd went on to Rotherham, whence they eventually reached the Scottish Border by way of Leeds. It was stated that the Highlanders hid a considerable sum of money near Redmires, but many subsequent searchers failed to find the treasure. It is a romantic local story, and the teller proudly owns the good George Worrall as great-great-great-grandfather, and sports the White Cockade. In this I bear her company, for I too own an ancestor, who marched with Bonnie Prince Charlie.

THE OLD COACH ROAD to Buxton from Sheffield, left by Psalter Lane and climbed to Ringinglow, crossed Houndkirk Moor and fell to Grindleford Bridge through Longshaw woods; then up the cruelly steep Sir William Hill to Great Hucklow and Tideswell, entering Buxton via Wormhill.

The branch to Manchester descended the Sy' gate to Castleton and up the savage Winnats Pass to Sparrowpit, thence to Chapel-en-le-Frith by the steep old lane near Slack Hall.

BROOKFIELD MANOR reached from Hathersage through its private park or more romantically by following the long winding lane that drops to Brookfield Bridge, hides an interesting past in its lonely seclusion. An old wing of the house bears the date 1646 and belonged to the day when outer defence was needful. The Gate House through the yard with its slit windows and archway hails from a bygone age, whilst the tiny prison with its low door and ruined roof stirs up a melancholy and damp speculation on the fate of felons condemned to durance vile for game trespass.

The extensive outbuildings of the north side are washed by the babbling brook ; the whole courtyard being strangely attractive and unusual for these parts. The gateway made me think of Dunster Castle in Somerset. Surely some history can be unearthed about this old manor house !

CORONATION BONFIRES were lit on the Peakland hills keeping up an old tradition that dates from Armada days, and probably long before that in times of danger. But this time it was a happy occasion in honour of our young Queen Elizabeth.

In spite of pouring rain the fires blazed bravely, twinkling their message of loyalty into the night sky from hilltop to hilltop.

Those of us who saw them or took part in the event felt it was one more bit of Peakland's long history.